"RELIC TRAILS TO TREASURE"

The Americana Price Guide

by

Wes and Ruby Bressie

Authors of

"Ghost Town Bottle Price Guide"
"101 Ghost Town Relics"

The Truth in History through Relics

Price $4.50

Published by

OLD TIME BOTTLE PUBLISHING COMPANY
Salem, Oregon

Printed in the United States of America

Library of Congress catalog Card No. 70–113427

SBN No. 911068–05–8

TABLE OF CONTENTS

ACKNOWLEDGEMENTS

We wish to acknowledge our sincere appreciation to the following collectors and museums for the many courtesies shown in allowing us permission to photograph material from their collections. We especially wish to thank Terry Skibby for his superior photography.

Our sincere thanks to Lynn Blumenstein, author, publisher, without whose words of encouragement this book would not have been written.

Jacksonville Museum, Jacksonville, Oregon
Wells-Fargo Museum, San Francisco, California
Brotherton Collection, Bonanza, Oregon
A.B.C. Shop, Wickenburg, Arizona
Terry Skibby, Ashland, Oregon
Harvey Smith, Hilt, California
Sam & Ruth Merriman, Merrill, Oregon
Chuck Jackson, Drew, Oregon
Ramsey Ghost Town, Ramsey, Arizona
Blossom Flury, Shady Cove, Oregon
Kerbyville Museum, Kerby, Oregon
Mert Thomson, Eagle Point, Oregon
Old Oregon Museum, Gold Hill, Oregon
Old Time Bottle Pub. Co. Museum, Salem, Oregon
Jim Hanscom, Phoenix, Oregon
Betty Surber, Medford, Oregon
Tex Shively Horn Collection, Salem, Oregon
Rosemary Barnes, Salem, Oregon
Ray Skibby, Ashland, Oregon

INTRODUCTION

The word Treasure means many things to many people. To some it may mean the re-discovering of a lost gold mine, a cache of jewelry or other valuables taken in some long forgotten stage robbery, or the finding of a half-rotted miner's poke of gold or silver coins. These large finds are rare, but one can have a sizeable treasure by accumulating many small finds.

With the use of a metal locator, many unpublicized Treasure Troves are being uncovered every day. Less strenuous sources for picking up early day items are the old estate auctions, Flea Markets and junk shops.

There are various types of collectors, with some it's just knick-knacks, while others choose salt and pepper sets. There are collectors of dolls, bottles, coins, match books, tokens, and old automobiles. It might be an old ore car, an 1857 Sibley Stove, a piece of early day barb wire or a tiny calico button, but there is someone, somewhere, that collects that particular thing.

"Things" in general have taken on a little more value. For instance the old tin tobacco containers were seldom seen in the shops and when they were, the price was usually a dollar or two. Now, the scene has changed nationwide. Collectors are clamoring for them and the value has risen. Depending on the condition, they range in price from $3.00 for one in fair condition in the common class, to as high as $75.00 and up for the rare ones.

Brass and copper powder flasks are another "hot" item in the collecting field. The embossing may include bugles, George Washington, hunting scenes, eagles, or just a scroll design. These old flasks are becoming increasingly scarce as new collectors enter the field, and this factor has helped in high values being placed on these once necessary and common items. They range from $30.00 to over $100.00 for the rare ones. Some of the manufacturers were Colt, Simpson, Ames and American Cap & Flask Company. Several flasks have been dug at old military forts and town sites. One in particular was found in the rock wall of an old building, untouched since put there by an old miner in the mid 1860's. This flask was in perfect condition.

Following up leads and studying the items found at a given site sometimes reveals the nature of the occupant; whether he was a spender or a thrifty person. The latter type would be more apt to hide his money, having no faith in banks. Watch for old landmarks, such as very old trees, rock outcrops, etc. It's surprising what a metal detector can and has uncovered in these areas. Other good places to use the detector are around old fireplaces, cellars, under stairwells, horse stalls and even old barns. Always remember that treasure was usually hidden within sight of the house.

Consideration of others is the most important thing to remember in treasure hunting. Never cross a "No Trespassing" sign. In case of private property, acquire permission from the owner, fill all holes and of course never destroy buildings.

Until recent years, little has been written on the subject of Relics and all the related treasures. Many of these much sought after items still lie stashed away and forgotten in some leaky barn or farmhouse attic, where they are being ruined or completely destroyed by that destructive little creature, the mouse.

The following pages contain photographs and hundreds of items priced to help give the collector some idea of the monetary value of "Treasure".

GHOST CAMPS

   Trails to the hidden and the discarded treasures of a past era lead to moss-covered homesteads tucked away in the hills, to railroad camps, and rock ruins of ghost towns. Some of these places are reached only by hair-raising jeep trails in the Colorado Rockies or by hiking miles of railroad track. Many of the rails are abandoned, with sections of narrow gauge rails and rotted ties lying helter-skelter along their routes.

   Many of these old camps have a feeling of serenity about them, as the evening sun touches the few remaining weathered buildings before it moves beyond the purple hills. Not all places have this atmosphere about them, however, there is that "certain something" about the old ghost town of Hamilton, Nevada. Located ten miles off the highway between Eureka and Ely, Nevada, the dirt road is easily accessible by car. Just before reaching the town proper, on a knoll to the left of the road lies the cemetery with it's many markers left standing. Some are of stone, while others were meticulously carved from wood, now leaning precariously. Some of the names are readable, others barely legible, and many completely eroded away by the wind and rains. Like most camps of the sixties and seventies, death claimed them young, from pneumonia, smallpox or sudden violence. These headstones are a monument to those courageous men and women who endured the hardships in a wild and untamed land.

   A short distance further and a veiw of what once was the town of Hamilton, Nevada appears with it's few scattered remnants of buildings and tumble-down rock walls. One can stand in the dust of main street and try to envision the town that is no more. On the right is the red brick Wells-Fargo building, still standing with it's roof caved in. In it's hey-day valuable shipments must have crossed over the rock threshold and through the huge iron doors. Across the street are the ruins of the Withington Hotel. Built of brick, it was originally one of the most spacious structures in the state, catering to the best clientele. On both sides of the street are the remains of other business houses, many of which were no doubt saloons as they usually outnumbered other establishments in these old mining camps. Behind several foundations were piles of broken bottles, most of which contained various brands of whiskey, ale or bitters. Drinking was the favorite pastime of the miners after a day of backbreaking labor in the mines.

During the winter, the elements played tricks and numerous storms were recorded at these above 8,000 foot elevations, with temperatures dropping to 25 degrees below zero making it necessary to keep fires burning in the cabins both day and night. Wood was scarce and for ten miles around the hills were stripped of every scrap of available fuel, hauled in on mule-back to be sold to the residents at high prices. Snowfall was very heavy at times. During one particular winter, snow was reported at a depth of eight feet in Hamilton, which brought travel of any sort practically to a standstill. Hamilton was not alone with her trials and tribulations as there is a roadsign pointing easterly to her neighboring sister towns of Eberhardt and Shermantown, Nevada. Shermantown may also be reached by the Treasure City road

Towering over all, like a silent sentinel is Treasure Peak and the rock ruins of Treasure City. This wind-swept town, aptly named, is likewise accessible by car. From bits and pieces gathered, a tale is told of the fabulous wealth taken from those dark yawning shafts. The miners worked long hours for approximately four dollars a day, spending one dollar of that for a dozen eggs. During the winter the miners often paid twice that amount for that needed nourishment. Cases of frostbite were numerous and in some instances there were frozen feet and fingers that had to be amputated.

An Aura of history hovers over the entire area and each relic found must surely have a story behind it. Some mementos can be found by patient searching and observing. A small amount of windblown sand or dirt can conceal treasure in the form of a coin, ox shoe, powder flask, or even an arrowhead. Recently a Plantation Bitters bottle was uncovered by merely flipping over a piece of tin inside the rock foundation of a building at Treasure City. The old bottle was completely covered with a beautiful soft white coating. Other bottles that were also revealed were black glass ale bottles, crock mineral water jug with handle and a tall graceful olive green bottle with a bulbous neck that is commonly referred to as a Lady's Leg Bitters. Also recovered were several coins in near mint condition. The coins were a seated Liberty, 1863s dime, 1865s fifty cent piece and an 1873cc quarter valued at over four hundred dollars. Two pistols in rusty condition came out of one hole. A derringer and a pepperbox firearm, four powder flasks and several bullet molds were also found in this area. One of the powder flasks was small and straight sided, heavily embossed with leaves and acorns. This particular flask contained two chambers, one for the powder and another for the balls. This flask was discovered wedged between the wall rocks of an old cabin, untouched since having been placed there by it's original owner many years ago.

Many other town sites, now lonely and unpeopled have yielded treasure of a sort. The West Coast has been the proving ground for the Treasure Hunter while such states as Texas, Florida, Kansas and Michigan have given forth memories that shall last forever.

Golconda Hoist Plant and Gold Mills

Stices Gulch Placer Mines No. 3

RELICS

Early 1900 jail located at Quartzite, Arizona

Handcuffs were recovered from the remains of an escaped murderer who had broken away while being transported to a New Mexico prison in 1912. The remains of the prisoner were found nineteen years later in the New Mexico desert.

Leg iron which is reminiscent of early day equipment used to restrain prisoners. Other types of equipment used were a long length of heavy chain with iron ball attached. During the period 1875–1909, the Yuma Territorial Prison in Arizona used a system where a ring was embedded in the floor with a short length of chain containing the leg iron.

Early day handcuffs, commonly referred to as "Come-a-longs".

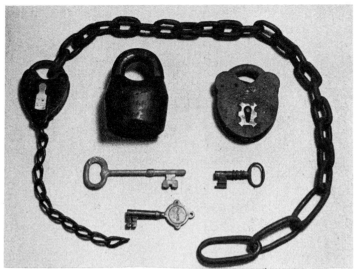

Left to Right: (1) Lock & chain recovered from old homestead site; initials on the swivel key cover signifies the manufacturer's name. (2) Lock is of the same style as was used at the old Walla Walla State Prison in Washington State in the early years. It has raised star around keyhole. (3) Tumbler padlock (4) Iron house key (5) Tumbler padlock key (6) "Palace" hotel key.

Left to Right: (1) Lock with brass keyhole cover used during the period 1860—1900. (2) Lock recovered from early Western townsite for the period 1850—1860. These were used on jails and store buildings. (3) Solid brass lock inscribed "Good Luck" on the horseshoe design. (4,5,6,7,8) Brass locks and keys of British manufacture. (9,10) Early day brass keys.

13

Strongbox was discovered in 1968 in the mountains of Northern Calif—
ornia at an abandoned mine site and was built of iron with sturdy
handles and reinforced walls. Knob and door hinges were made of
brass.

Saddle received it's name from General George B. McClellen, commanding officer in the Union Army and is of Hungarian design.

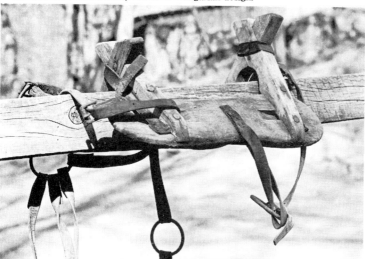

Pack saddle referred to as a Rocky Mountain Crosstree or Saw Buck pack saddle. It was used in the early days when mule pack trains were the life-blood of the gold camps and early settlements.

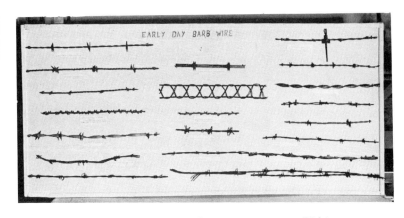

Left	Center	Right
1. Thorney Fence 1868	1. Stubbe Plate 1883	1. The Winner 1874
2. Split Diamond 1875	3. Wrap Around 1878	5. Two Point
4. Champion 1880's	5. Four Point 1877	7. Buckthorne 1881
5. Brink Twist 1879	6. Left Hand Twist	
6. Chain Link 1884 (machine)		

UTILIZATION — Coffee Table: Wagon wheel hub mounted on disc blade with attached solid rubber tired wheel which has been glassed in across the top.

16

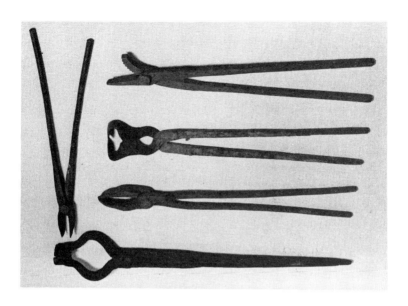

TOP: Blacksmith tongs

BOTTOM: (Top Left) Bench Plane. (Top Right) Spoke Shaver. Was to smooth out the spoke and shape it for the wagon hubs. (Center) Boring auger. Was used in making holes in the hewed logs for a wooden pin. (Bottom) Molding Planes.

17

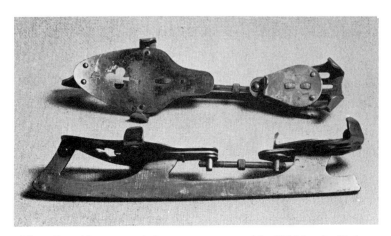

The adjustable cast steel skates were patented in 1894 by the Union Hardware Co. of Torrington, Conn.

American Parlor or Floor Skate in relic condition. ca. 1865

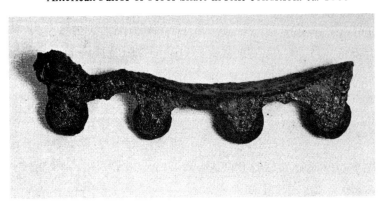

Newhouse bear and varment traps.

The first trap manufactured in the United States was made by Sewell Newhouse in Oneida, New York. Newhouse began in a small factory with less than half a dozen employees in 1855, however, in 1872 he was employing nearly 300 workers

Two clamps used for setting a bear trap.

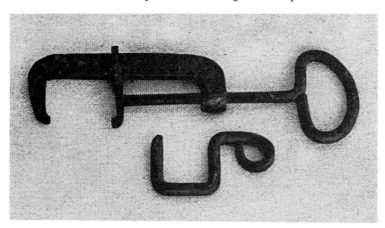

All metal seal. The Daniel Land Co. Oregon, Incorporated May 18, 1907

Pencil Point Jupitern. Favor Guhl & Co., New York. Made only by Guhl & Harbeck, Hamburg, Germany. Guhl & Harbeck Original Machine. The pencil holder slides back and forth on a bar, adjusting to the length of the pencil. By turning the wheel on the right, small cog-like blades sharpen the pencil point.

TOP
Bee Smoker. The bellows is pumped, forcing smoke from the spout, then out
from the spout of the metal fuel container, onto the bees.
BOTTOM
(top) Rip or Pit saw (1860's) A couple of short logs were laid across a
long narrow pit. The log to be sawed was laid on them, with one man in
the pit and another standing above. The log was ripped into lumber by
pushing the log across the smaller logs and sawing up and down. (center)
Cross Cut saw. (Bottom) Broad Axe.

21

Hand forged Cooper's Adz used for making and repairing casks and
barrels.

Top to Bottom: Wooden carpenter's plane. Inscribed: "Edward
Carter", Troy New York. Draw Knife

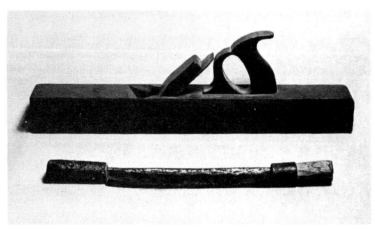

Old tin powder keg. (Base reads "Pacific Mills Powder."—Top reads "Pat. March 31, July 12, 1857–59".

Small wooden barrel   Early plow

Early Wooden Barrel

Wooden Mauls. Were
used in driving fence
posts.

Wooden wheelbarrow. Made from barrel staves.

Wooden wheelbarrow. Made from flat boards.

TOP: Reed Lunch Pail—Top closure is a tin drinking cup, while a metal tray inside was for sandwiches. The bottom half of the pail was used for liquids. BOTTOM: Ships Lantern — It was designed to fit in a corner, having a metal slot—hook that fit on a bracket. Glass over light is blue.

TOP: Old grindstone for sharpening scythes, knives, etc. This machine was run by sitting and pedaling to turn the grinding wheel. The can or container over the wheel held water that dripped onto the grinder. Patent date on the grindstone is August 7, 1899
BOTTOM: Case Knives, lower right inscribed "Old Sunny Brook Brand Whiskey"

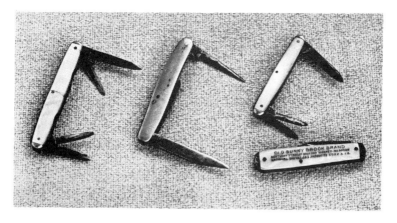

27

Train caboose lamp

Water pipe—the pipe was wrapped metal and hand-riveted, was found at Marietta, Nevada. Pipes from similar construction made of leather and hand-riveted have also been found.

Brass spikes recovered from 1849 ship wreck. Coins, Spanish Pieces of Eight date 1714 taken from early ship wreck off the coast of Florida.

28

Beehive shaped sandstone
Match Holder & Striker from
Table Rock Saloon in
Jacksonville, Oregon

Sandstone Match Holder
& Striker, excavated on
Rock Creek near Sheridan,
Oregon.

Copper Whiskey Still (from Prohibition days)

Cast Iron Heating Stove ("St. James Bonnet & Nance, Quincy, Ill.")

Bellows (were pumped by hand to give air to the embers in starting a fire.)

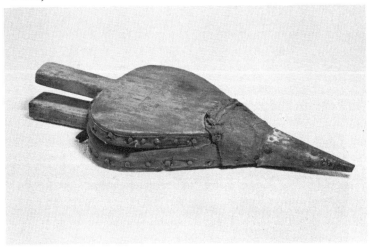

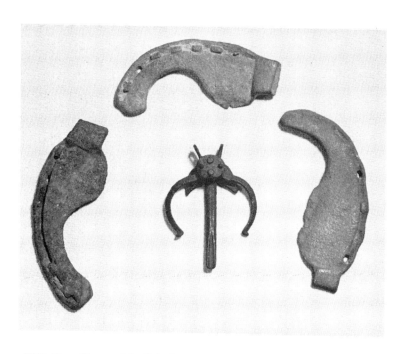

TOP: Oxen Shoes and Ox Yoke Pin. Oxen shoes were made in two pieces to fit the cloven hoof. When shoeing an oxen a sling was brought into use, as his three legs would not support his tremendous weight if shod as one would a horse. BOTTOM: Spring Wagon

Ornate Spanish Spurs. Large spur was found still strapped to a portion of a boot with parts of a human leg bone scattered around it.

Hand forged Spurs

The Chileno or Ring Bit was used to curb half-wild or unruly horses. The ring most usually had a small chain attached that went down under the jaw and attached to the shank of the bit.

Hand Carved Stirrup   Iron Boot Jack in the shape of a Beetle

A pair of hand carved stirrups.

SIBLEY STOVE

In 1857, Major Henry Sibley procured a patent on this tent warmer designed for the use of troopers while in the field. There was a four inch pipe attached to the small end of the stove and run out through the top of the tent. The draft was regulated by scuffing dirt against the small hole at the base. The one pictured is the thirty pound model, used by the enlisted men. There was also an eighteen pounder designed for the officer's quarters. This particular stove originally came from old Ft. Klamath. Later versions were of machine manufacture and of welded construction, while the older ones were hand riveted.

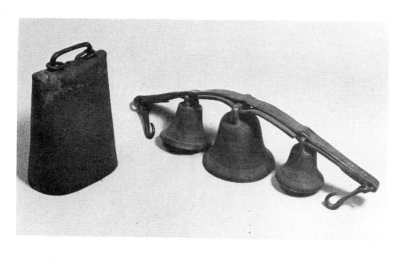

Left to Right: Cow Bells and Freight Wagon Harness Bells.

"The New-Era Rope Machine." Mfd. by A. D. Long, Fairfield, Iowa,
July 18, 1911

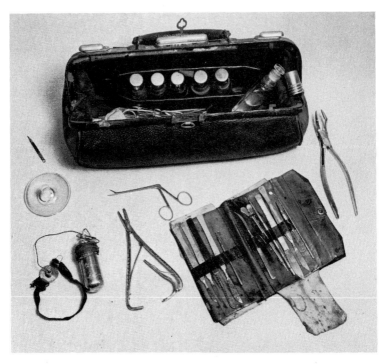

TOP: The black leather Doctor's satchel holds many early instruments, some similar to those being used today. The instruments consist of forceps, several tweezers, scalpels, hypodermic needles, bottles that still smell of Lysol and a blown glass nineteenth century breast pump.
BOTTOM:
Early Doctors Medical Kit

Wooden Harness repair bench

Portable iron Hitching Blocks. They were carried in the buggy and especially used in the Doctor's buggy. The blocks were dropped "Overboard" when a regular hitching post was not available.

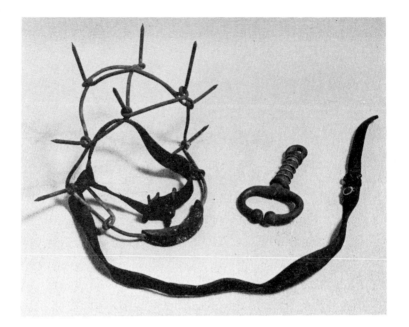

Left to Right: The spiney looking halter is a Calf Weaner. If the calf got too near the mother, the calf would be quickly expelled.

Cattle leader. This was put in the nostrils and a rope in the small loop to lead with.

Hay Knife

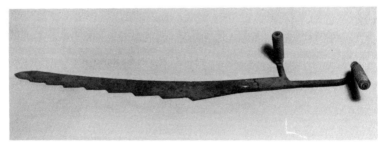

Wooden Hand-Fashioned Bootjacks

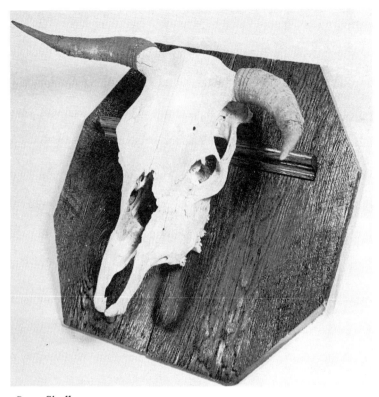

Steer Skull

Buffalo Skull

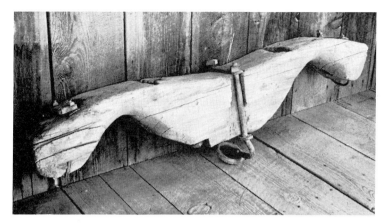

Ox Yoke, Minus Bows

Left to Right: (1) Round bottom bucket that hung under the wagon (2) Wagon wheel hub. (3) Tin container held "Hub Brand Axle Grease" for wagon hubs. Embossed on lid is a picture of wagon hub. This was put up by the "Brininstool Co. Los Angeles, California. (4) Buggy wrench. (5) Hub nut wrench

Cast Iron Waffle Iron

Ram Pump

Early 1900 Coleman Lamp

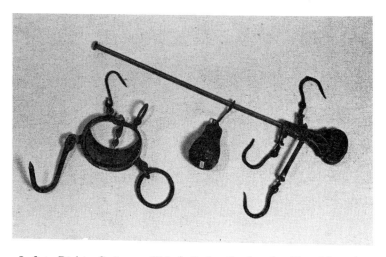

Left to Right: Cotton or Hider's Scale. Steelyard or Portable scale.

Left to Right: Meat hooks commonly used in smoke houses.
Staples — this size was normally used in conjunction with a hook as
on a gate or barn door.

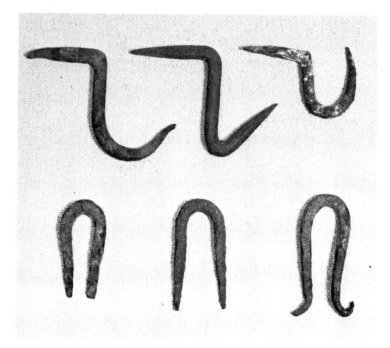

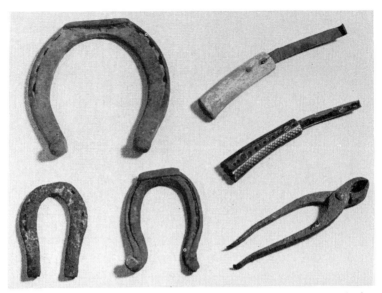

Shoes: Large horse shoe is for a work horse, medium shoe is for a regular size horse, small shoe is for a burro. Knives: Top to bottom, Farrier's knife or hoof reamer, Metal knife is dated 1898, Blacksmith's pincers.

STODDARD'S LIGHTNING TIRE UPSETTER (Instructions for use)
The small center lever should be fastened up, leaving the eccentrics raised and ready for use. Heat the tire to a soft heat, place the hot part under the clamp in the opening to prevent tire from kinking. Bring down the small lever in front, so that the eccentrics are pressed firmly to the tire; let go small lever and bring down long lever, and upset to amount required. Then raise long lever first to loosen tire.   Tire measure hanging upon wall.

Early buggy steps

Bar bits for horses. The center right bar bit has five links resembling a bicycle chain only sharper; a wicked restraining device used on hard to handle horses.

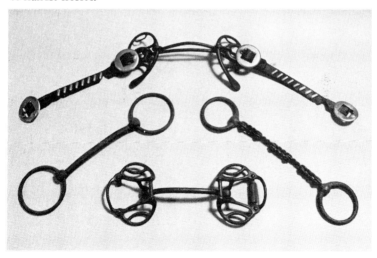

The auto lock was patented in 1914 and is complete with key. A small brass plate reads, "This car is protected by Security Auto-Theft Signal System." Model T Wrench

Early state license plates

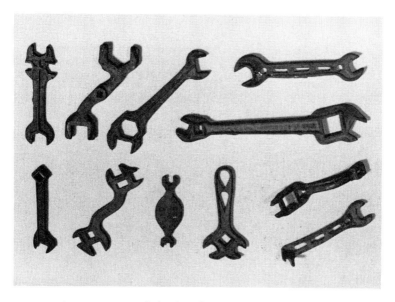

An assortment of obsolete farm equipment wrenches.

Early wagon jacks

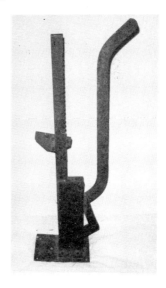

RELIC ODDITIES

A variety of articles have been discovered entombed in old trees. An old coffee grinder was found half-embedded in a tree in the mountains near Darwin, California. Horseshoes, barb wire and square nails have also been recovered from within trees. Old insulators have been observed protruding from very old line trees.

Implements such as wedges, axes, branding irons and even an old cross cut saw have been observed in this phenomenal position. Rifles, early day miner's picks and gold pans are some of the relic examples that have been found.

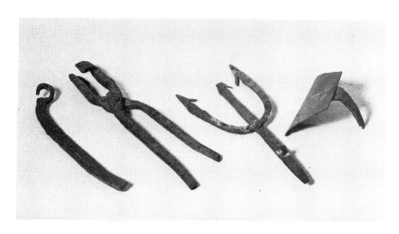

These roughly made implements are one of the best representations of our pioneer ingenuity. These historical objects were hand fashioned from cast off horseshoes making them "one of a kind" relics.
Left to Right: Wrench, Blacksmith Tongs, Salmon Spear or Harpoon, Hoe - this hoe was hacked from a flat piece of metal into a rough shape of a hoe, and to this was hand-riveted a horseshoe on which the handle was affixed.

Left to Right: Bootjack, Iron Ring, Trap Drag

TOBACCO TINS

Some of the most interesting decorated tobacco tins were "Surbrugs Golden Sceptre" 1861 and Mayo's "Constellation" in 1891. Mayo also put out a clever and a highly desirable tin in a shape similar to the fabled children's character, "Humpty Dumpty".

J. G. Dill's "Best Cut Plug" came in a yellow and green flat tin with a picture of a lady inside an oval frame. This tin dates back to 1891. Dill's tobacco was also put out in a tall rectangular tin with hinged lid.

P. Lorrilard, America's first tobacco company, was established in 1760. Some of their tin examples includes "Just Suits", "Climax", "Golden Twins", "Sensation", "Tiger", and "Union Leader". The Union Leader tins come in several styles: The lunch pail type with bail displaying an Eagle standing on a package of tobacco, the round humidor type with a picture characterizing "Uncle Sam" smoking a pipe, also, the flat tin.

In 1881 Tiger Chewing Tobacco sold in one ounce foil packages which was put up in five and ten pound boxes. The purchaser had the option of buying tobacco in boxes or in decorated tin containers at a slightly higher cost. In 1914, "Tiger Bright", and "Dark Chewing Tobacco" was available in decorated tin canisters, containing 48 packages of Tiger in five cent paraffin bags.

The R. J. Reynolds and the American Tobacco Companies also made colorful tins. Strater Bros., a branch of the Burley Tobacco Co. were manufacturers of "Satisfaction Cut Plug" tin in the lunch pail design.

TOP:
Left to Right: (1) Gold Shore Cut—Plug Tobacco in the lunch pail design; hinged lid, gold letters on white. (2) B. F. Gravely's Best Flue Cured Plug Cut. Hinged lid, rectangular, flat. (3) Satisfaction Cut Plug. Hinged lid, snap type latch, small bail handle, gold letters on red. (4) Lucky Strike, R. A. Patterson Tobacco Co., Rich'd, Va. was put out after the Civil War by Dr. Richard A. Patterson who had been a Doctor in the Confederate Army. This came in a flat tin with hinged lid and black letters on red circle with a green background. (5) Oriental mixture, a High Grade Tobacco. Rectangular shape, hinged lid. Silver, yellow and red tin.

BOTTOM:
Left to Right: Union Leader Tobacco. "Uncle Sam" smoking pipe. Round container, white on red and press-on lid. (2) Union Leader Tobacco in flat, tall tin. Hinged lid. (3) Catcher Rough Cut Pipe Tobacco. White on Orange. Pipe on blue. Round tin, press-on lid. (4) Early clay pipe. (5) J. G. Dill's Best Cut Plug.

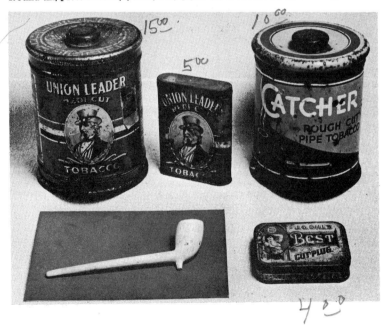

Iron Tobacco Cutter

Tobacco Humidor

53

Brass Cuspidor

Granitewear
Cuspidor

China Cuspidor

THE MINER

MINER'S TABLE SETTING

The cheap soldered tinware was lightweight for packing into isolated areas and served the miners immediate needs. Found in mining camps of the 1860's.

The small coffee pot has a slender slot in the side with glass inset to see the amount of coffee inside and the pouring spout starts at the base of the pot. The coffee cup handle is hinged.

Both the bone and wooden handled knife and three tined fork were used during this period.

The small cans contained baking powder and had holes punched in the lids to be used for shakers.

The bowl and plate were also made of tin.

Kerosene or Coal Oil tin containers minus spouts. circa 1860–1870. Far Right, Galvanized kerosene container of later vintage.

Left to Right: Wide flared tin bowl. Tin tea kettle with copper base was made to set in the hole after the stove lid was removed. Small tin pail with bail has soldered seams.

Left to Right: The round tin lunch pail was the standard size and shape used by the early miners up till the period near the turn of the century when the rectangular shape appeared. They have a round tin sleeve on the lid over which the drinking cup fits. The flared mixing bowl has holes punched in it's bottom to be used as a colander. Large coffee pot has crudely soldered seams.

Left to Right: Small Log Cabin Syrup can with soldered seams is an early version. Large Log Cabin Syrup can is a later version with soldered seams. Labeled Log Cabin Syrup can is a crimped seam version, ca 1930's. Small tool was used for removing screw top closure.

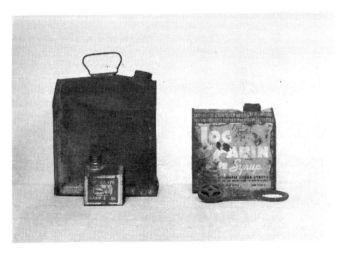

TOP: Dry Washer for the recovery of gold. The pay dirt was shoveled onto the slanted top riffle board with screen or a sieve beneath. The heavy material was caught here with the finer part going through, then moved on through still another screen to catch the fine gold. The large nuggets would naturally be caught on the first level.

BOTTOM: Gold Rocker for the recovery of gold with the use of water. The box is mounted on rockers and is worked back and forth to sift the gold bearing dirt through the perforated bottom of the box onto a riffle board beneath. The heavier material stays in the box.

59

Pottery assaying crucibles. Miners hand forged shot hole cleaning tool. For cleaning drill hole before setting explosive charge.

Various assay crucibles

Scarce, heavy duty miners pick

60

Gold Scales, Circa, 1850

Left to Right: (1) Early miners lamp. The spout contained the wick and possibly used whale oil as fuel. (2) Miners pick in relic condition. (3) Early gold pan with 3½ inch lip as compared to 4 inch lip used on modern gold pans. (4) Miners tweezers for removing gold nuggets from bedrock.

Ore car used in the early mines. It ran on a track into the mine drift where it was filled. The bed tilted up with a lever that opened one end of the box for dumping. Engraved on a brass plate is the manufacturers name. "F. M. Davis Iron Works Co., Denver, Col."

Large ore bucket with heavy iron bail. Manufacture: "The Mine & Smelter Supply Co., El Paso, Denver & Salt Lake City."

Left to Right: Miners candle holder. Pointed end was stuck into mine wall crevice, while metal band held candle. (2) Miners carbide lamp. Early versions of the carbide lamp were quite ornate and were attached to the miners head piece. (3) Scissor instrument is a wick trimmer. (4) Early lantern which used coal oil or kerosene as fuel.
Bottom picture: Miners Picks. Top to Bottom.   Mattock. Drift Pick. These miners picks have been recovered from various mining sites dating between 1860 to 1900.

Left to Right: Mercury Flask (quicksilver) Flask contained 76 lbs. when full. Quicksilver is extracted from the ore cinnabar with the use of a Retort. One of the many uses for Mercury is in the recovery of gold. Pan crucible. Iron pan was used in assaying. The bottom of each cubicle is pointed.

Canteen measures fourteen and one half inches. Recovered at Newark, Nevada

INSULATORS

Left to Right: (1) A "Mulford & Biddle," threadless glass insulator dated before 1865. This type of insulator was held on the wooden peg or pin by first wrapping a piece of burlap around the end of the pin, coating it with red lead, then forcing the insulator over it. (2) A rare olive green E.C.&M. Co. S.F. One of the first threaded types made on the West Coast in 1871. They have been found in cobalt blue, green, blue-green and the rare olive green colors. (3) Later vintage of the "Cutter Pat. April 26, 04". The "Cutter" was not too satisfactory as the wire lay in the glass "saddle" and many times a limb falling across the wire would snap off the glass C shaped projection.

An example of how the E.C.&M Co. insulators were used. No cross arms were used and only one insulator to the pole. The insulator sat directly on top of the pole attached to a threaded peg. The wooden peg was counter-sunk into the top of the pole, with an inch wide steel ring driven over the pole. This ring was then held in place by a hand-forged square spike, compressing the peg in a secure position.

66

Left to Right: (1) Embossed on rim: "CHI. INS. Co., PAT. OCT. 16, 1883".
Turquoise blue in color. (2) Embossed on front "CALIFORNIA". Light
honey or yellow in color. (3) Embossed on dome: "H. G. CO." Embossed
on skirt "PETTICOAT". Peacock blue in color.

Left to Right: (1) Embossed upon dome: "W. E. MFG. CO." and near base
is PATENT DEC. 19, 1871. Reverse: W. U. B. Blue green in color. (2)
Embossed "CALIFORNIA". (This insulator is referred to as a "hot cross
bun", because of the indented cross in the top.) Brownish amethyst in
color. (3) Embossed "HEMINGRAY 25" (unusual shape) Blue green in color.

Left to Right: (1) Embossed: "CALIFORNIA PAT. APL'D FOR." Smokey green in color. (2) Embossed "HEMINGRAY 109". Reverse: MADE IN U.S.A. Blue green in color. (3) Embossed: "PYREX T M REG. U. S. PAT. OFF." Reverse: MADE IN U.S.A. 63. Carnival glass color.
Below, Left to Right: (1) Embossed: "BROOKFIELD". Blue green in color. (2) Embossed: "HEMINGRAY NO. 1 PROVO TYPE" Reverse: PATENT MAY 2, 1893 (This insulator is often referred to as a "Hoop Skirt") (3) Embossed: "REGISTERED TRADE MARK" (with emblem) Reverse: PATENTED JUNE 17, 1890. Blue green in color

Left to right: (1) Embossed: "HEMINGRAY PATENT MAY 2, 1893" (two piece — twelve inches high) Blue green in color. (2) Embossed: "HEMINGRAY 25" (four inches high) Blue green in color. (3) Embossed: "VICTOR DEC. 11, 1900. PAT. NOV. 24 & DEC. 15, 96. SEP. 28, 97. JUNE 7, 98. F. M. LOCKE, VICTOR, N.Y." (two piece with porcelain top, eleven inches high.) Brown & aqua in color. (4) Embossed: "HEMINGRAY NO. 79". (three piece) Blue green in color.

Wells-Fargo & Co. organized in 1852, also brought about the American Express Company. Wells-Fargo operated up and down the Pacific Coast and throughout the Mother Lode country of California, carrying mail into remote areas to settlers and miners alike. Wells-Fargo was known all over the West and handled more bullion and silver than any other Express Company. They finally merged with Railway Express Company in 1918.

WELLS FARGO

Left to Right:

Freight Receipts dated 1895. from the Alameda, California office to Oroville, California. Receipts read: "Company's Lines cover 38,000 miles extended over Railroad, Stage Lines and Steamboat routes."

Cancelled checks issued by Wells-Fargo at Carson, Nevada (not Carson City) on May 15, 1885. Second receipt down dated 1888. Bottom receipt reads 1874. Pay to Wells-Fargo & Co., from the National Gold Bank & Trust Co. of San Francisco.

Pony Express way station in Nevada showing the transfer to a fresh mount.

Courtesy Wells-Fargo History Room, S.F.

WELLS FARGO

THE PONY AND THE WIRE

Two romantic events closely associated in the progress of the west was the Pony Express and the Overland Telegraph.

Mail service was extremely slow in the 1850's, having to come by ship around the Horn, thus involving weeks and even months of waiting. To improve this situation, an ingenious plan was formed by Russel Majors and Company, to start what was to become the famous Pony Express. The Pony Express was to be inaugurated on the third day of April, 1860. In the meantime, men, horses and equipment would have to be obtained and distributed over the designated route.

The following information has been compiled from old newspaper articles relating the events leading up tb the start of the Pony Express and the Overland Telegraph.

This advertisement appeared in the Sacramento Union on March 19, 1860:

"Men Wanted. The undersigned wishes to hire ten to a dozen men familiar with the management of horses, as hostlers or riders on the Overland Express Route via Salt Lake City. Wages $50.00 per month. Signed, Wm. W. Finney."

About two hundred young men reportedly responded to the advertisement and the required number were hired. Wm. Finney completed arrangements for stocking the portion of the route assigned to him and started his men and animals for distribution along the route. He purchased one hundred and twenty-nine mules, also, tents for those stationed beyond Carson Valley. Twenty-one men as express riders and packers were distributed between Sacramento, California and Eagle Valley in Nevada. The line beyond this was stocked westward from Salt Lake City, Utah.

In the beginning the stations were twenty and twenty-five miles apart. Later, some stations were only nine and ten miles apart. The terrain was the final deciding factor on how far each horse could travel. They would travel from one station to another twice a week. Each rider was to ride from thirty-five to seventy-five miles, using several horses to accomplish the distance. Two minutes were allowed to change horses at each station and the riders averaged about nine miles per hour.

On April 14th, in preparation for the appearance of the first Pony from the East, various devices and quaint signs began to appear in front of the stores on J street in Sacramento. Flags were hung from awning posts and the Loryea Crockery Shop even had a hobby horse mounted and decorated with flags. Dale & Company across the street dressed their largest doll and mounted it on a wooden pony, placed papers in it's hand, a cap on it's head and added in large letters, "PONY EXPRESS FOREVER". Many similar slogans appeared up and down the street. The streets along the route of the Pony Express were lined with excited spectators; balconies were filled by the ladies in their colorful gowns. Everyone strained to catch a glimpse of the first sign of the rider and his pony. At long last all the preparations and tense waiting was rewarded. A cloud of rolling dust appeared, then a horseman surrounded by mounted citizens. Bells from church towers and fire engine houses rang a welcome amidst the roar of the crowds and the boom of a cannon. The little pony stretched his neck and raced down the dusty street that was wild with excitement. Here and there were rider-less horses, while others were out of control of their riders. Out of the confusion and cheering emerged at last the Pony, trotting up to the door of the Agency to deposit it's precious mail. The entire trip had taken just ten days from St. Joseph, Missouri to Sacramento, California. Two little flags adorned the headstall of the Pony, and from the pommel of the saddle on each side hung a bag lettered, "Overland Pony Express." The saddle was broad, the stirrups were of wood with immense flappers to guard the rider's feet. The young rider, dust covered and sun browned, was clad in buckskin and from his slim hip hung a 36 calibre Navy Colt cap and ball pistol. Thus the much glorified Pony Express was born.

During it's short reign, the first pony became a legend as the one who sped across sandy plains and mountains. It was said that he scared whole tribes of Indians, who believed he was an arrow whittled in the shape of a pony. The Indians swore he made the eagles heart-sick as his flight was so swift.

The express stations were hardly established before the Indian troubles began. They stole all the stock from the Dry Creek station in Nevada. As a precaution all the stock was brought from Sand Springs to Millers in Carson Valley. On June 15th, the last Pony going East was turned back at Dry Creek. The body of the station keeper was found and all the animals at the Simpson's Park station were missing. Nothing was heard from any of the stations beyond Sand Springs as the Indians had cut them off. A reward of $100.00 each was offered to a company of twenty-five men to go through to Salt Lake to reopen the route.

In September an immigrant train arrived by way of the Pony Express route and reported that Indians were numerous. The pony was of great value in protecting immigrant trains as the riders carried news between trains enabling them to guard against attacks.

During this time the Directors of the Western Union Telegraph Company were holding meetings in the East, trying to decide a route for the construction of the much needed Trans-continental telegraph line.

In April, 1861, the Pony Express Company transferred it's office and contents to Wells-Fargo and Company, located on Second Street in Sacramento, California. Also in April, the California State Telegraph Company filed a certificate of incorporation "for the purpose of constructing and working lines of telegraph."

In the month of May, a man by the name of James Street was appointed general agent for the Overland Telegraph Line. His job was to make arrangements for getting out the poles, purchase the needed teams and make all the provisions for construction of the telegraph line. This line was to eventually spell the end of the Pony Express route.

In mid-May, five wagons marked "Telegraph Wagons" were received at Sacramento, California. Each wagon had a long "reach" to extend it for hauling the telegraph poles. James Street left Sacramento with an outfit consisting of fifteen wagons, one hundred and fifty head of oxen and the necessary riding horses to begin the construction of the telegraph line between Carson Valley and Salt Lake.

On June 22nd in 1861, the first pole on the Overland Telegraph Line was erected, extending east from Ft. Churchill. On July 13th, the first telegraph pole in Utah was planted on the main street in Salt Lake City. By September the lines had been extended from Salt Lake City westward to Ruby, Nevada where a station was erected. No further extensions were made until the wires, insulators and batteries were procured. The holes were dug, however, the poles were another matter.

There was great difficulty in procuring the poles for the line sixty some odd miles to the east of the Ruby Station. A wagon train was engaged in delivering poles over the desert from Simpson's Park to Deep Creek, a distance of about sixty-six miles. From the canyons where the poles grew, to the extreme western edge of the desert where the poles had to be transported, was approximately one hundred sixty hot, weary miles. Both animals and men suffered greatly from lack of water. Oxen and mules were used in delivering and distributing the poles. The ox teams started after sundown from Simpson's, traveling over twenty-two miles onto the desert where each deposited it's load. They then would return to Simpson's without rest or water, managing to reach there before noon the following day. The seventeen mule teams remained on the desert distributing the poles where food and water had to be taken to them daily. Two four-mule teams were constantly engaged at Simpson's Springs hauling barrels of water to those distributing teams. Men and animals became practically dehydrated working unsheltered beneath that blistering inferno, the desert sun.

On October 23rd in 1861, the Great Overland Telegraph connection was made. The message first sent was to Abraham Lincoln from the Chief Justice of California, Stephen Field. The connection meant the end of the Pony. On October 25th, the now famous Pony Express, no longer needed, was discontinued ending another colorful era in the building of the West.

Wells Fargo Bank History Room
San Francisco, California

Pictured above is the "Mochila" or saddle bags, made of leather and used by the riders on the Pony Express. The Mochila slipped over the saddle with a slot for the saddle horn and cantle making a sort of saddle cover. The Mochila had four pockets, called "Cantinas", two on each side in which the mail was placed. Three of these pockets were kept locked from the point of origin, and opened only at Military Posts and Salt Lake City. The fourth pocket was for way stations, with each station keeper having a key. A time card of the departure and arrival had to be filled out at each station and carried in this pocket.

      The same Mochila was used from the time the rider left his Western or Eastern terminus. The maximum weight allowed was twenty pounds and $5.00 was the original charge, plus regular postage, providing the weight was kept to one half ounce or less.

Wooden Telegraph Insulator from the first
transcontinental telegraph line across
Nevada. Circa 1861

LEVI STRAUSS PRINT

During the latter part of the Gold Rush period, Levi Strauss came to San Francisco and realized the need for work clothes of rugged durability. He produced
what the miners needed and became famous. Levis is a name that remains a
byword today for fine Western wear. The pictured print is on cheese cloth,
faded and worn, showing years of having hung in the old ranch house. In the
upper right hand corner is the Trade Mark, Patented May 20th, 1873. The
print dates around the turn of the century according to the cowboys' regalia.

THE GHOST OF OLD FORT DATE CREEK

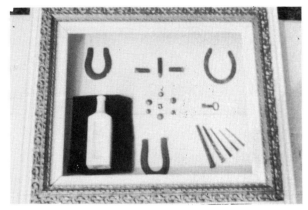

Old maps of Arizona will reveal the location of several early army posts which are scattered throughout the state. Some of these are in a state of preservation, while others are past restoring and lie forlorn and forgotten in the desert. One of these abandoned outposts lies approximately eight miles off the highway between Congress and Prescott, and situated on a rolling sandy knoll, it commanded a good view of the surrounding area.

In early spring, the brilliant crimson splashes of the Fairy Dusters or red-tipped Ocotillo are beautifully in bloom, and in many washes grow the colorful desert gourds.

A dusty road cuts through the center of the fort, abandoned and untended. The rain and wind has melted the buildings into nothing, merely flat outlines appear where once stood adobe walls. Originally called Fort McPherson, the name was changed to Camp Date Creek on July 15, 1867. The camp was moved several times, returning always to Date Creek. It originally stood on the north bank, but was moved to the south bank of Date Creek in 1868. The buildings enclosed a quadrangle parade ground with the men's quarters, the butcher and bake houses on the north. The officer's quarters were on the south, the guardhouse on the east, and the post hospital on the west. Water was carted from the creek in barrels and ran through charcoal filters.

Down along the banks of the creek to the north are still partial remains of rock walls, hidden by a screen of Palo Verde trees. Around this area are bits and pieces of metal, also horseshoes and horseshoe nails, even a grey wild burro hiding in the sagebrush. Throughout much of this part of Arizona roam bands of these small animals, once the companion—helper to the lonely prospector; the same prospector and miner for which the fort was originally designed to protect. It's purpose also was to protect the early settlers on the La Paz to Wickenburg Road and to guard the mail from Prescott to La Paz on the Colorado River. In 1868, Capt. J. W. Weir was the commanding officer of the 14th cavalry in charge of companies "H" and "I".

Scattered over the entire camp area are various sizes of hand-forged nails, rusted pieces of soldered-bottom tin cans, parts of crudely blown bottles, and necks of rare whiskey flasks in yellow-greens and golden ambers. The broken thin panes of colorful blue-aqua cathedral pickle bottles and bases with their rough iron and broken pontils are strewn over the sand. Since the desert seems to preserve certain metals and wood, some of the items that have survived for nearly a century are brass uniform buttons embossed with eagle and shield, smaller buttons with the letter "I" in the center of the shield, signifying one of the companies stationed at the fort, or a small brass number that was worn on the cap, old unmarked rim-fire shell casings, 50 calibre Sharps, and bullets of 45 — 70 calibre.

History of these old forts unveils itself through the form of a tiny army button, age—old shell casings or a soldier's belt buckle.

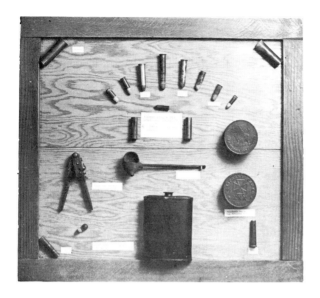

Relic Board: A Relic Board for displaying small objects such as
old shell casings, bullet molds, lead ladles, powder cans and
California Cap Co. cans.

Framed Relics, Top — Left to Right: (1) Powder Horn (2) Bullet
Mold for ball and slug (3) Colt's patent brass powder flask with
a small Eagle design.
Bottom — Left to Right: (1) Scroll design flask for rifles (2)
Colt pistol (unmarked) 31 calibre cap and ball. (3) Small object
is a Teat-Fire shell casing for front loading revolver. (4) Bullet
mold for a ball. (5) Colt's powder flask for Colt Belt (Navy)
pistols.

Top: This 38 calibre Iver Johnson was found under the walk of an old home stead. Left: 32 calibre "American Double Action" forerunner of Harrington & Richardson. Right: 32 calibre Iver Johnson with spur latch.

Sixshot Pepperbox

Unknown

Derringer

Old Rifle dated 1864 ("W. T. Howell & Co."

Early Rifle (Belgium made)
Powder Flask. (Engraved Hazard Powder Co.")

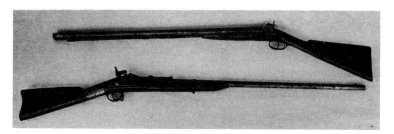

Double barreled 12 ga. shotgun. "Henry Proryn—London."
U. S. Springfield 58 calibre 1863. (Has a brass band engraved with the name "Mefe". Note: These two guns were supposedly used in the Modoc War of 1873

22 calibre single shot "Hopkins & Allen" with falling block action. Twenty three inches long and is considered rare as a Trapper's gun.

Painting of an Indian Brave done in transparent oils by Jeanne Bressie
This was taken from an old pillow cover. These pillows were sold as
souvenirs of the Buffalo Bill Wild West Shows.

INDIAN ARTIFACTS

Top to Bottom: Smoking pipe carved from sandstone. Medicine man's Fetish. (A rattle made of hide with painted symbols.)

Left to Right: Clay Bowl, Hudson Bay trade axe made of steel, Glass trade beads, Ancient Indian Skull.

Cradle Board is of Split Bamboo and was used to carry a Papoose. (rare)

Left to Right: (1) The "Mano" or rubbing stone was used in conjunction with the Metate for mashing or grinding grain for flour. (2) Stone Indian Club. (3) Grooved stone shaft smoother. (4) An assortment of thimbles, buttons and brass bracelet. Small holes were drilled through the thimbles and worn as a necklace.

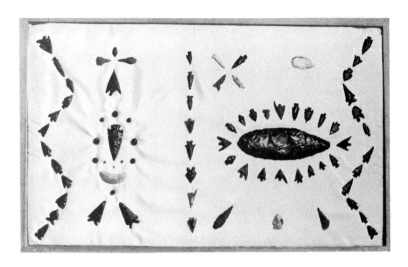

Arrowhead plaque display of obsidian, jasper and agate. The crescent shaped object on the left is of yellow agate and is an ornament or possibly a medicine man's fetish. Around the arrowhead above it are eleven Trade Beads. Around the large scraper on the right are several Rogue Points made of jasper.

Most of the points in the center are Rogue Points. The larger spear pointing down is of gray and white agate material. This plaque is also comprised of scrapers, spears, and arrowheads of jasper, obsidian and agate.

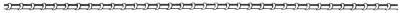

Two scarce Indian baskets

Left to Right: Large polished & fluted axe used in making canoes. Columbia River Tomahawk. Polished granite War Club. (three inches long)

POWDER HORNS

Traveling Horns

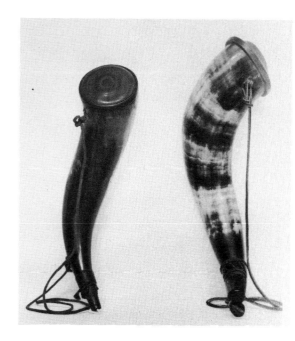

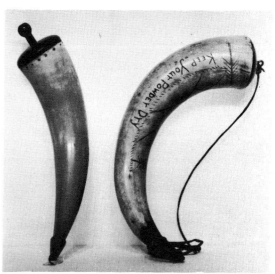

Left, Hunting Horn

Right, Traveling Horn

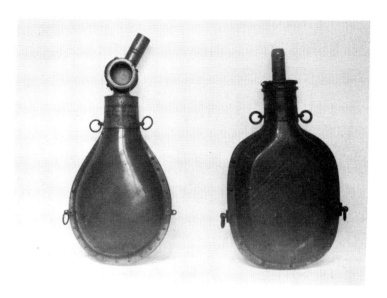

Left to Right: Visible Charger (tortoise shell), Adjustable Charger (tortoise shell)

Top, German Flat Horn (spring charger) Bottom, Adjustable Charger

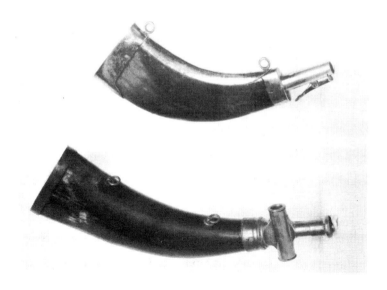

Bottle Flasks

Adjustable Chargers

Left to Right:
Rifle Horn
Flintlock Priming Horn

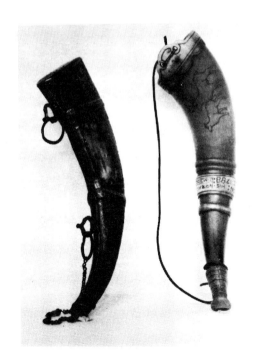

Left to Right:
Arabian Horn,
Flintlock Horn
(signed Simon Kenton)

Shot Gun Adjustable Charger

Colt Navy Bent Spout Flask
circa 1861 – 1865

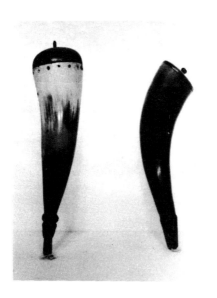

Rifle Horns (small bore)

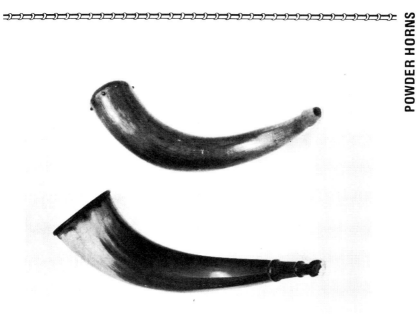

Early traveling horns

Historical rifle horns

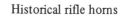

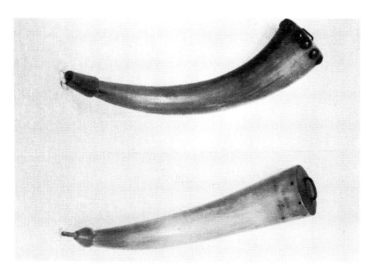

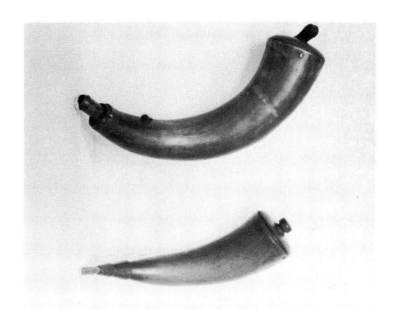

Top to Bottom: Traveling Horn (adjustable charger) Small Hunting Horn

Top to Bottom: Bottle Flask (tortoise shell), Flaten Horn (common primer)

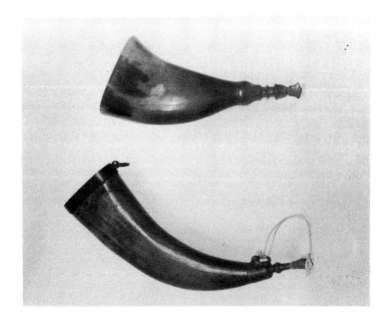

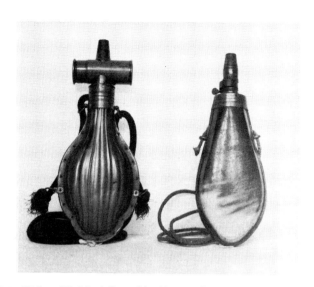

Left to Right: Visible Adjustable Charger (tortoise shell), Horn Flask (bottle type)

Left to Right: Adjustable Charger (signed "Boche"), Early Flask, (heavy brass overlay)

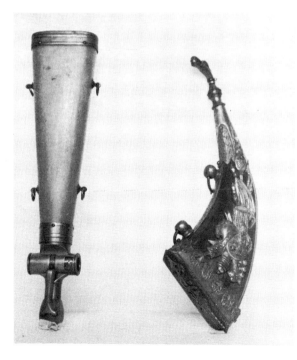

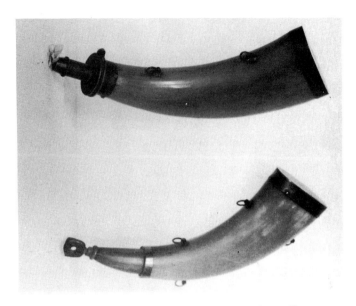

Top to Bottom: Adjustable Charger, Flaten Horn

Top to Bottom: Adjustable Charger, Priming Horn

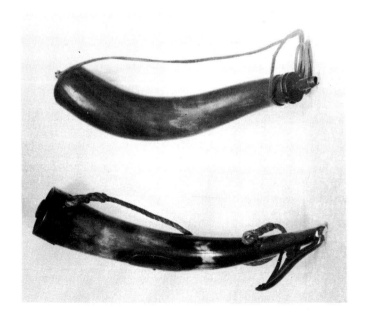

Left:
Spring Adjustable
Charger (rare)

Right:
Rifle Horn

Left:
Rifleman Horn

Right:
Paneled Horn

97

Left to Right:
Colonial Storage Horn
English Army Horn

Left to Right:
Rifleman Horn
Pistol Flask Horn
(Adjustable charger)

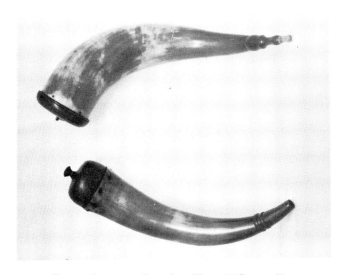

Top to Bottom: Traveling Horn, Rifleman Horn

G.A.R. Whiskey Flasks

Left: Horn Cups, Far Right: Snuff Box

BOTTLES & ETC.

Original Old Label Display

Commercial Sign (company was formed in 1893)

Left to Right: Beer Tray, Humboldt Brewing Co., Eureka, California, 1913, Coaster Tray, Beaverhead Brewery, Dillon, Montana

Left to Right: Ramsay's Superior Scotch. Dupar McCullough & Plimpton, Salida, Colo.

Beer trays, left to right: Wielands Extra Pale Lager, Unmarked Beer Tray

Left to Right: Wooden Bottle Corker. Cork Screws. Corker is hinged in the middle and the bottom section has a tapered brass liner. The corker sat on top of the bottle and the cork was compressed through the liner into the neck of the bottle with the aid of the wooden plunger.

Pineapple shape bottled (J. C. & Co., Color Amber.)

Left to Right: (1) Frank Abadie. Wholesale Liquors, Eureka, Nevada (2) Quaker Maid Whiskey. S. Hirsch & Co. (3) Ceramic bottle (often referred to as a "Snort". (4) Cork Screw (Old Kentucky Home Club U.P.S. Whiskey, Blumauer & Hoch Wholesale Liquor Dealers. Sole Agents. Portland, Oregon

Left to Right: (1) Case Bottle (Cosmopoliet, J. J. Melchers, Schiedam.) (2) Beer Bottle (Crystal Brewage, Baltimore, Md, U.S.A. (3) Personal flask (marked G.D.)

105

Left to Right:
(1) Val Blatz Brewing Co., Denver, Colo. Blatz Brewing Company had a branch in Denver in the 1890's
(2) Rainier Beer. Seattle Brewing & Malting Company. This company was formed in 1893. Emil Sick absorbed the company and still uses the trade name "Rainier".
(3) H. Weinhard, Portland, Or. In 1860 Henry Weinhard acquired a brewery in Portland, Oregon, which is still a family business.
(4) Little Fauser. U. S. Lager. (porcelain stopper reads: John Fauser & Co. U.S.)

EARLY 1700 – 1800 BLACK GLASS

EARLY 1700 – 1800 BLACK GLASS

Left to Right: Casper's Inc. Winston Salem N.C. N.Y. Chicago, St. Louis. ca. 1902–1906. Color: Cobalt Blue. Home brewing bottle. Glass pocket was for holding sediment while pouring, machine made bottle, Color: amber.

Left to Right: Chestnut Bottle, ca. 1860's Color: golden amber. (pontil) Early American Flask) Color: Sapphire blue. (rare)

Left to Right: Onion (Black Glass) bottles. Seal reads: Lo" ALLEN 172

Left to Right: Early Flask (front & back view) Cobalt blue in color

110

Left to Right: Fruit Jars. (1) Mason's Patent Nov. 30th, 1858, Aqua in Color (2) Globe (amber in color) (3) Lightning, amber in color (4) Atlas Mason's Patent Nov. 30th, 1858 Aqua in color.

Left to Right: Steam Cooker, Toledo Cooker, patented Feb. 5, 1907; Drey, Aqua in color; Root Mason, aqua in color; Mason's Patent Nov. 30th, 1858, aqua in color.

Left to Right: SUN TRADE MARK. Base embossed: J. P. BARSTOW, Apple Green in color. (crown) TRADE MARK FULL MEASURE REGISTERED QUART. Base embossed: A. G. SMALLEY & CO. BOSTON & NEW YORK. PATENTED 1896, Amethyst in color. TRADE MARK ELECTRIC. Aqua blue in color. GEM (Maltese Cross) Base embossed: PAT. NOV. 26, 67. Aqua in color.

Left to Right: MASON'S PATENT NOV. 30th, 1858. Amber in color. COHANSEY, Aqua in color. WOODBURY, Base embossed: W.G.W. Aqua in color. MASON'S FRUIT JAR. Aqua in color.

CHINESE ITEMS

Three small Chinese bottles (left to right) (1) The sheared lip bottle is a beautiful green color (2) Center bottle contains the original medicine. (3) This bottle contained poison and is six-sided, cobalt blue in color.
Below, Chinese medicine bottles (left to right) (1) The tear drop shaped bottle dispense just one drop. (2) Banjo shaped bottled contained tiny pills. (3) The double bulbed bott is unique. (4) Many of the long necked ones had a number near the base.

114

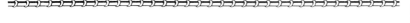

Chinese Containers: The small glazed pottery jugs and the larger one were for preserving food or spices. The square one held Soy Sauce. Chinese soy sauce usually came in a round container with a tiny pouring spout. This one is unusual in the fact that it is square. They normally came in brown and bluish glazes and sometimes in an orange type color, with various designs on the shoulders. 1870–1880 period.

Chinese Tiger Whiskey. Middle jug is a later version, ca 1935–1963.

Chinese Scales: Weight measurements on ivory stick. Weight is achieved by sliding metal disc along ivory stick until correct balance is established. Complete with bamboo case with embedded brass chinese characters on lid. Used for weighing gold, opium, etc. Below: Brass Chinese lock and keys. The key fit in the end of the lock. The other end slid out, exposing three prongs in it's base and the top prong.

116

This unusual heavily decorated Chinese Relic is made of brass and is a pressing iron. The cup was filled with hot coals.

Brass ladle from old Chinese mining town. The metal turner has "China" inscribed on it.

Saloon, Chinese Joss House, Silver City, Idaho.

HOUSEHOLD

LORAIN WOOD STOVE

Stoves such as this were the center of the family. Many a childhood memory evokes a picture of the kitchen, bright and sunny in the summertime and warm and cozy in the winter. Such thoughts also bring to mind the spicy smell of warm gingerbread, fruit pies baking in the large oven, or roasting turkey filled with it's aromatic dressing. Somehow the "good times" at home are usually associated with the family suppers in the kitchen and the old wood burning cook stove. With these warm thoughts, the inconvenience of filling the wood box is forgotten. The reservoir top was also a very good spot to set the bread to rise, and the warming oven over the stove was handy for keeping both the plates and food warm.

Left to Right: (1) The wooden butter churn is over 100 years old, and made of vertical slats with metal bands that hold them tightly in place. (2) The dasher is made of wood also. (3) The tall tin churn with tin lid is a "Reed's" patented in Nov. 1890. Most every family of any size had their own cow and churned their own butter. Many times the chore of churning was given to a younger member of the family, leaving the older ones for heavier jobs around the house. The final phase of butter making was turned over to the mother or older daughter. She in turn removed it from the churn, patted it into a ball, squeezing out all the cream, and molded it, whether by hand or with the use of a butter mold. The molds were usually of wood, some having fancy designs cut in the wood to be molded into the butter.

The barrel type with crank made the chore of churning a little easier, but did not lessen the monotony of it. The "Cylinder Churn" when cranked, turned the barrel, churning the butter as it turned.

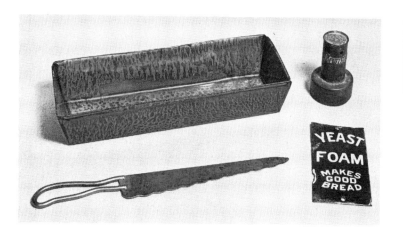

Top, left to right: Long bread pan made of gray granite ware, "Rumford's soldered tin doughnut cutter. Bottom, left to right: All metal bread knife, Small white on blue enameled sign. "Yeast Foam Makes Good Bread."

Left to Right: Universal food chopper. Chopper has four knives. The fine for sausage, mincemeat and hamburger, etc. The medium is for fish and poultry. The course is for hash, hog's head cheese and vegetables for stews. The chopper also contained a nut butter knife for making butter from nuts of an oily nature.
(2) The Arcade Flour Mill. A domestic necessity for grinding flour from any small grains.
(3) The Arcade Coffee Grinder is a later version with glass holder for the coffee beans.

Left to Right: Large cast iron skillet with long applied handle. This is typical of the skillets used in cooking over a campfire or in a fireplace. Cast Iron Pot (early version)

Left to Right: The cast iron dutch oven is minus it's lid and was used by the Chuck Wagon cook. Small pancake griddle was found at a ghost town site. Wooden and metal grater.

Red Jacket Mfg. Co. water pump. A product of Davenport, Iowa

Classic Fruit & Lard Press

123

Left: Wooden
Lemon Squeezer
with porcelain
bowl

Right: Metal lemon
squeezer

Tin Match Box Holder and Striker. Advertises: "Telephone 54 for Herman
Stormer. Undertaker on Eighth, between K & State, Quincy, Ill" in gold letter

Left to Right: Utility jug, brown and white in color. Utility jug made of gray glazed pottery. "Weir" jug for preserving foods, etc. ca. 1892

Ice Tongs

Left to Right: Gray graniteware cream container. Milcan Coffee, Closset & Devers, Portland & Seattle

Left to Right: Poppy Marshmallows. Yellow poppies on blue background Happy Home Peanut Butter. Rock-A-Way Oysters. Reverse: Gentleman seated at table dressed in a tuxedo eating oysters from the shell. Tao Tea Balls. Silver on black in color. Picture of dragon on press-on lid.

126

Iron Tea Kettle. These kettles were kept on the back of the stove filled with water. The kettle was made to fit in the hole by removing the stove lid. These kettles were enameled white inside and had a swing lid.

Left to Right: Cast Iron Muffin Pan. Cast Iron corn bread pan. Cast Iron muffin pan.

Left to Right: Salt Cellar, Stoneware Pitcher (recovered from old townsite, dating in the mid-1800 era. Long handled wooden spoon.

Left to Right: Can Opener. Patented July 25, 1893 by A. S. Co. of Columbia Lemon Extract Bottle. Wooden butter mold with Swan design. Early soldere tin scoop

Left to Right: Hoosier Kitchen Cabinet. Early spice bottle, ca 1850–1860. Wooden lemon squeezer. Raisin Seeder, Enterprise Mfg. Co. Philadelphia, Pa. U.S.A. Pat. Apr 2, Aug 20. '95 & Oct. 5, '97 "Wet the Raisins". The seeders claim was to seed a pound of raisins in five minutes.

Cherry Pitter. N. S. Hdwe. Wks. of Mount Joy, Pa. The pitter was called the "New Standard Cherry Stoner."

129

Left to Right: Soldered seamed tinned cake pan. Gray enameled Tea strainer Gray enameled colander.

Left to Right: Soldered seamed tinned coffee pot. "Rumford Measuring Cup Soldered seamed cup advertised "Rumford Baking Powder." "For Household Use only." Quart size with soldered seams. Tinned grater. Patented Aug. 6,

Left to Right: Tinned Egg Scale. Columbia Family Scale. Pat'd. April 16, '07.
Put out by "Landers, Frary & Clark" of New Britain, Conn.

Left to Right: Combination funnel and cookie cutter. Tinned with soldered
seams. Tin candle holder. Has lever on side to push candle up   as it burned
down. Ice cream scoop.

The Cobbler's tool box contains a complete set of implements for repairing or replacing soles on shoes.

Utilization of relics.

Fireplace Poker Stand

Left to Right: Small iron with detachable handle. "Sensible No. 6. N.R.S. & Co."
Metal Trivet for holding hot iron. Peak Coffee. "Freshly Roasted. See it ground
fresh for you."

Left to Right: Portable heater with wick called "Brightest & Best." with flat iron
on top. Large charcoal burner iron. Patented 1852 by "W. D. Cummings & E.
Bliss." Small charcoal burner iron. Patented by "Peppas & Alex Co. Cleveland,
Ohio. No. 2"

133

Iron Cauldron with three legs.

These large pots were used for washing clothes, scalding hogs and rendering lard, etc.

Large Lard Press. Measures four feet in height.

Left to Right: Early adult chair with leather sitting portion. Child's high chair, ca. 1873.

Early American bathtubs were made to represent a slipper, on the same order as those used in Europe. The one pictured is of light metal and of the same design as those made in 1805.

Early day door knobs

Early hinge and lock plates. Hinge at top left is a screen door hinge, dated 18?

Ornate Brass Bed

Chamber Pot. "Ironstone China. Meakin, England"

"Clipper Lawn Mower"
Pat. Nov. 9, 1895,
August 18, 1900

Left to Right: Oaken Bucket. Ladle. "Buckeye Force Pump", Mast Foos & Co
Springfield, Ohio

Left to Right: Tin eight hole candle mold. For making long tapered
candles. For making candles a wire or stick was laid across the top
of the holes. To this a cotton thread was tied and ran down through
the molds for use as a wick. The tallow was then poured into the
molds. After the tallow hardened, the mold was then dipped into
hot water to loosen the molded candles for removal. (2) Tin
Coffee Mill. (3) Wooden Coffee Mill.

Commercial type
coffee mill.
"Enterprise Mfg.
Co., Philadelphia
Pa". Pat. Oct.
21, '73

DOLLS, TOYS, ETC.

Wicker doll buggy complete with black parasol, wooden wheels and hubs, ca 1900. Doll is a bisque head with paper mache body and is called "Kaiser Baby".

DOLLS. These dolls are referred to as "Frozen Charlottes", and date from 1840 to the turn of the century. Those with painted on features are glazed china and the others are stone bisque. A long poem was written on the fabled story of the dolls. The story is about a young girl named Charlotte who disobeyed her mother by not dressing warmly enough when riding to a ball on New Years Eve, 1840. The young girl froze to death.

"PENNY DOLLS" are stone bisque and only the wired on arms are movable. The clothes for these tiny dolls were usually made from pieces of colorful ribbons in various widths. These dolls were favorites of little girls.

141

Doll heads (before 1860)

Dolls may be dated by their hair styles and types of shoes. China heads are glazed-over bisque. Flat-top hair styles and high foreheads are before 1860, as are the legs with flat soled shoes. Heads with more elaborate hair-do's and legs with high heeled shoes are after 1860.

Doll heads (after 1860)

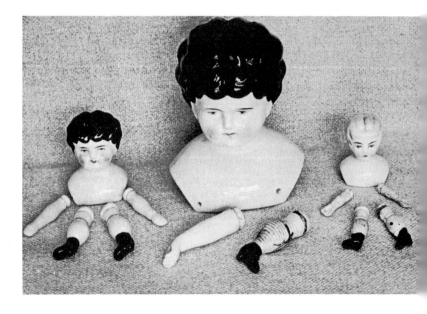

Doll Trunk

Early doll and clothes (reconditioned)

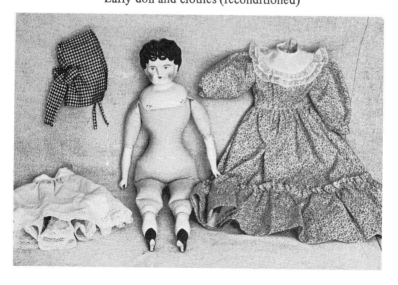

DOLLS, TOYS, ETC.

Left to Right: Cast iron Bear Bank. These banks were peddled throughout the country by a group of Latvian Missionaries to raise traveling money in the 1920's. Cast iron Castle Bank.

Buttons. The jet black button with anchor design was found at a site called "Sailor's Digging."

144

Cast Iron Toys

"Beauty" Childrens cook stove

Children's shoes. "Linen Nursery Book". Advertises the Hanford Mfg. Co. products. Hanford's Balsam supposedly cured lameness, deep cuts, burns, stiff neck and sore throat. Book copyrighted 1905.

MARSHALL FIELDS

1888

WHOLESALE CATALOG

GAMES.

No. 536½. Fish Pond Game, new and improved. The finest game of Fish Pond ever offered at a popular price. It contains patented features; is gotten up in the very best manner wtih very handsome labels and with the best of implements. ½ doz. package...............per doz., $2 00

Our new and desirable Fish Pond Games. (Patented.)
No. 535. Improved Game of Fish Pond. Extra fine edition......per doz., $8 00
No. 536. Improved Fish Pond Game. Fine edition. ½ doz. package......per doz., 4 00

No. 452. Golden Locks Series. Size, 10½x20 in. Three kinds, assorted, in quarter dozens. Little Golden Locks, Little Red Riding Hood, Jack the Giant Killer. The Golden Locks Games are the largest and handsomest ever offered at the price. The boards are laid flat and fastened in the bottoms of the boxes, and are, consequently, of the same size as the boxes. This is a form adopted last season for the first time. It has proved very satisfactory.........per doz., $4 00

No. 692. Diamond series. New. Three kinds put up, assorted, in quarter dozens. Cats and Mice and Tousel. Captive Princess and Ambuscades. Life's Mishaps and Bobbing around the Circle. This series is compiled from the old Favorite Series, revised, corrected and improved. The best of the old games have been selected, new and very handsome labels have been designed, and the boxes doubled in size. The series is designed for children; per doz., $4 00

No. 328. Leatherette Lotto. Size of box 9¼x7¾ in. It is of wood, covered with imitation of alligator skin leatherette of the color and appearance of Russia Leather. The title and an ornamental design are stamped in gold on the lid. The box contains a large box of glass, a set of 90 well finished lotto men, and 24 lotto cards............per doz., $5 35

No. 521. Geographical. An educational game. An excellent edition, from which those who play it will find in condensed form most of the important facts concerning the geography of the world. An excellent amusement, especially adapted for the use of schools, as well as the home circle. ½ doz. in package.
...............................per doz., $4 00

Trunk Box Lotto—design patented. Lotto is one of the very few games which grows into popularity year after year. It is so simple and easily learned that very young children readily master it. It provides a fund of constant interest and amusement, and does not become the least bit monotonous.

No. 417. ½ doz. in package, per doz., $2 00
"   418. ½   "   "   "   4 00
"   419. ¼   "   "   "   6 75
No. 327½. "American" Lotto, Black Box, ¼ doz. in package, per doz., $4 00

148

GAMES.

No. 529. The Battle Game. Box contains one large army gorge-ously arrayed, and fully officered, with toy pistol, etc., and full directions. A showy and desirable game......per doz., $8 00

No. 509. Great Battlefields. The only game treating of this subject. Elegantly printed on fine cardboard. Exceedingly entertaining and giving instruction upon events interesting to people of all ages. It is well that all young people should know the great generals who have fought the famous battles of the world. Played on the book system with certain copy-righted improvements. In box with battle scene on the il-luminated label. ½ doz. in ackage...............per doz., $2 00

No. 506. Billy Bumps' Visit to Boston. This new humorous reading game has a very large sale; the book describes Billy's adventures and experiences in his journey to the "Hub," the accompanying cards fill in the blank spaces, in a manner calcu-lated to make young people very merry, per doz............................$2 00

No. 507. Johnny's Historical Game. One of the most pleasing and instructive games on our list, and one that should be played in every home, by young and old. The great events of national history are, by its use, firmly fixed in the mind, per doz.................................$2 00

No. 513. Young People's Geographical Game New 1890. A carefully prepared and excellent game. A good geographi-cal game always meets with a ready sale, both with the young folks themselves and with their parents, handsomely is-sued at a popular price.......per doz., $2 00

No. 500. The Game of Luck. A most interesting game of pure luck and chance, comes with spinner on top, counters and full directions. Very exciting........................per doz., $2 00

No. 501. A simple, pleasing little game of skill. The game is to seize the ball and convey it safely to a goal by moves, each side moving alternately. ½ doz. in package.........per doz., $2.00

TOYS.

No. 180. Farm Wagon, length 16 inches..per doz., $9 00

GATHMANN TORPEDO GUN.

A neat model of the most powerful weapon of war of the day. It is entirely harmless as a toy, no explosives or powder being used; rubber bands are used to furnish the propelling power. The torpedo is upheld in its flight by wings which guide and balance it, keeping it straight in the air. It will hit the mark.

No. 1. Cannon 11 inches, nicely mounted...............................per doz., $ 8 00
" 2. " 15 " U. S. Navy pattern .... " 16 50

Two torpedos, four bullets and a ship target are with each cannon.

PASTIME.

Toy base burner stove, transparent red windows, candle stick inside; base, top and urn nickel plated, one joint of pipe with each stove. Size of base 5¼ inches in square. Total height 12½ inches..........per doz., $9 00

No. W. Extra large, heavy Artillery; horses mismatched in color, gun carriage and limber dark green, red striped, gun dead black, brass mounted, men in uniform, length of toy 34 inches...per doz., $48 00

No. 409. Flying Artillery; brass cannon, 2 running horses, driver and odd rider; size 24x6½....................................per doz., $27 00

150

IRON TOYS.

No. 93. Pony Wheel Toy; length, 9 inches; height, 5½ inches; width, 3¼ inches. As the toy is drawn, each revolution of the wheels causes the driver to strike the pony with the whip. Handsomely painted in fancy colors; ⅙ dozen in package, per dozen.. $4 25

No. A. Sulky; horse black, harness gilt trimmed, sulky black, gilt striped, driver in jocky costume, length, 9½ inches, per dozen $4 25

No. B. Dray; horse black, harness gilt trimmed, dray wheels red, sides and front green, gilt stripes, load one box; length, 11½ inches...per doz., $4 25

No. CC. Dog Cart; horse black, harness gilt trimmed, cart yellow, wheels red and striped.......................per doz., $4 00

No. E. Surrey; horse brown, harness black, gilt trimmed, hip blanket buff, surrey body black, seats buff, gear black, red striped, driver in livery, length 15 inches...........per doz., $9 00

No. 175. Pony Express Wagon; length 14 inches.......per doz., $8 50

No. 185. Model Cart; length 13½ inches...............per doz., $9 00

No. 1. Single Truck; horse black, harness silver trimmed, collar and housings red, truck gear red, black striped, side stakes green, panels and foot board red, gilt striped, load, 1 box, barrel and sack; length 14 inches.................per doz., $9 00

151

IRON TOYS.

No. 1000. Fire Engine; painted in bright colors, horses black, driver in uniform, 16½ inches long and 6¾ inches high.
....per doz., $8 50

MODEL HOSE CART, No. 155.

Length 10½ inches, with rubber hose..................per doz., $5 50

Fire Engine No. R. Horses black, harness gilt trimmed, harness and housings red; engine gear red, black striped, nickel plated boiler and valves, body green and black, gilt striped, brass bell, gauge and whistle, engineer and driver in uniform; length 18¼ inches..................per doz., $20 00

Hose cart S S. Horse white, harness black; hames and housings red, cart body green, gilt striped, gear red, black striped, panels, seat, footboard and inside of reel red, length 15¾ inches......................................per doz., $13 50

MODEL FIRE ENGINE No. 125.

Length 19 inches...per doz., $18 00

No. 40-5. Mechanical Fire Engine, extra large, 2 running horses, driver, fireman and sectional hose; when wound 2 small wheels and the pump work rapidly imitating an engine at work at a fire; size, 19x7x5...per doz., $33 00

IRON TOYS.

No. 170. Fire captain's wagon, 12½ inches long,
5½ inches high....................per doz., $7 50

No. 135.   Model Hose Cart, length 15 inches........................per doz., $ 8 50
" 135½.   Same as No. 135, with rubber hose, length 15 inches........... "   10 00

No. 0. Fire Chief's Wagon. Horse white, harness black, hames
and housings red; body of wagon red, gear red, wheels red,
black striped; driver in uniform ....per doz., $13 50

No. P.   Fire Patrol, horses white and black, 18 inches long, wagon
body light blue, gear white, driver and three firemen in uniform ....per doz., $20 00

No. 1010. Hook and Ladder Truck; 2 ladders, horses
black, men in uniform, 24 inches long, 7⅓ inches
high......................................per doz., $9 00

Hook and Ladder No. T.   Horses white, harness black, hames and housings red; gear red, black striped, body black and green, with gilt
stripes and ornamentations, four red extension ladders, which can be
united, making a ladder, 51 inches long, 2 axes with red handles,
men in unifo.m; length of toy, 29 inches................per doz., $20 00

No. 130. Hook and Ladder Truck, length, 32 inches...per doz., $18 00

153

IRON TOYS.

Engine House V; size 26½x10x18; canvas roof, wood and malleable iron...per doz., $39 00

No. M. Contractor's Wagon; horses, black; harness, gilt trimmed; hames and collar, red; wagon—box, blue, gilt letters; gear, red; wheels, red, black striped..............per doz., $20 00

Tally-Ho. Galloping horses, harness, metal figures; length, 18 inches; per dozen...$54 00

No. D. Hansom, horse black, harness silver trimmed, hip blanket maroon, hansom black, panels yellow, with red stripes, driver in coachman's livery...................................per doz., $9 00

No. 190. Model Landau; length 16½ inches, finest iron horse toy ever made...per doz., $13 50

No. KK. Pony Phaeton; horse, white; harness, gilt trimmed; hip blanket, maroon; phaeton—body, black; seat, maroon; mat, orange; gear, red, black striped; wheels, red, black striped; lady driver.............................per doz., $10 50

No. L. Express Wagon; 2 horses, driver and wagon, painted in bright colors; load, 2 boxes, 2 barrels, 1 sack; length 17½ inches...per doz., $20 00

No. J. Double Truck; horses black, harness gilt trimmed, harness and collar red, truck gear red, black striped. side stakes green, gilt striped panels, seat and footboard red; load, 2 boxes, 2 barrels, 1 sack; length 17½ inches.............per doz., $18 00

IRON TRAINS.

47. Railroad Train, locomotive, tender and passenger. 10 inches long, 2½ high...........................per doz., $2 00

No. 40. Railroad Train, locomotive and tender, gondola car, brakemen on cars, length 18 inches.................per doz., $4 00

48. Railroad Train, locomotive, tender and passenger car; 14 inches long, 2½ high.....................................$2 75

No. H. Railroad Train; locomotive—boiler, black, gilt bands; wheels, red; stack, red; tender—black, bronzed wheels; car, red, black striped; wheels, black; caboose—red; wheels, black; total length 25 inches...........................per doz., 4 50

ɔ. G. Railroad Train; locomotive—boiler, black, gilt bands; wheels red; stack, red and black; brass bell; cab—maroon, gilt striped; tender—black, bronzed wheels, gold number; cars—red, black lettered; wheels, black; 34 inches long...........................per doz., $9 00

o. 43½. Locomotive and tender, two passenger cars, combination car, brakemen on cars, length 33 inches......................per doz., $9 00

ɨo. 70. Train, locomotive, tender, combination and passenger car; 38 inches long...per doz., $13 50

No. F. Passenger Train; locomotive—boiler, black; wheels, red; stack, red; bell, etc., gilt; cab—black, gilt striped; tender—black, gilt striped and lettered; car—red, black striped and lettered; 28½ inches long..per doz., $9 00

No. F. F. Railroad Train, locomotive, tender, combination and passenger car, finished in correct colors, 45 inches long........ .....per doz., $15 00

No. F. F. F. Locomotive—boiler, black, gilt trimmed; wheels, red; stack and domes, red and gilt trimmed; brass bell and frame; cab—black, gilt striped; tender—black, gilt trimmed and lettered; wheels, red; buffet car—olive green, gilt trimmed and lettered; ventilators and wheels, red; vestibule coach—olive green, gilt trimmed and lettered, ventilators and wheels, red; 60 inches long.....per doz., $66 00

155

BELL TOYS.

No. 24.   Bellringers; half size cut....................per doz., $3 75

No. 4.   Chime, with horse; 6½ inches, ½ dozen in package, per dozen $1 75

No. 15.   Half size cut; ⅓ dozen in package ....per doz., $1 85

No. 39.   Half size cut; horse swings on pedestal and rings the bell..per doz., $4 00

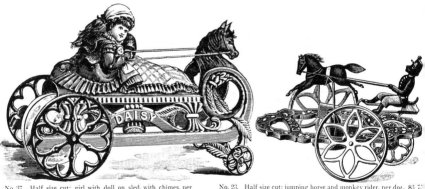

No. 37.   Half size cut; girl with doll on sled, with chimes, per dozen $4 00

No. 23.   Half size cut; jumping horse and monkey rider, per doz., $3 75

156

BELL TOYS.

No. 7. Half size cut, ⅓ dozen in package........per doz., $3 75   No. 38. Half size cut, Dog and Cat fight...........................per doz., $5 00

o. 27. Half size cut. $3 75

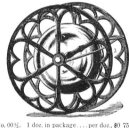

No. 00½. 1 doz. in package....per doz., $0 75
"   1½. ½ "   "   ....   "   1 75
"   2½. ½ "   "   "   4 00

o. 29. Half size cut...per doz., $3 75   No. 35. Half size cut, ⅓ dozen in package, per doz., $1 85

157

TOY BANKS.

No. 200. Nickel-plated security safe deposit, with brass combination lock and patent money guard. Size, 4¾ inches high, 3¾ wide, 3½ deep..per doz., $7 50

No. 119. Home Savings bank. Height, 6 in.; width, 4½ in.; depth, 3½ in. ¼ doz. in package, per doz..$2 00

National safe deposit bank with coppered combination lock and patented burglar-proof attachment. Finished in black and copper bronze. Size 6 in. high, 4½ in. wide, ¼ doz. in package...........per doz., $4 00

Junior safe deposit bank with coppered combination lock and patented burglar proof attachment. Finished in black and copper bronze. Size 4⅝ in. high, 3¾ in. wide. ½ doz. in package...........per doz., $2 00

No. A. Full nickel-plated, burglar proof, combination lock capable of 900 changes, 6¼ in. wide, 6 in. high and 4 in. deep...................per doz., $9 00

TOY BANKS.

No. 8. Half doz. in package, size
3¼ x 2½ x 2¼....... per doz., $0 75

No. 15. Height, 4¼ in., width, 3 in., depth 3 in.;
quarter doz. in package .... per doz., $2 00

No. 35. Watch Dog Safe, with combination
lock. Height, 6 in., width, 4¾ in., depth,
4½ in. When deposits are made the
watch dog barks. Beautifully finished
in gold bronze and colors...... per doz., $8 50

No. 400. Size, 6 inches high, 4¾ wide, 4¾ deep. New and accurate
combination lock, also has attached to the slot a patented
money guard, which will make the abstraction of money an im-
possibility. It is fitted up with a handsome oak cabinet, containing
two drawers with nickel trimmings. It is finished in black japan,
relieved with different shades of bronze. Packed one in a wooden
box .... per doz., $9 00

No. 150. Security Safe Deposit. Size 4¼ inches high,
3 wide, 3¾ deep. With brass combination lock and
patent money guard. It has a different style of
combination lock from regular safes, consisting of
one movable dial only which is turned forward or
backward to certain numbers. Full particulars will
be given on a tag accompanying each safe. Beautifully finished in nickel only. Packed three in a box.
.... per doz., $5 50

159

TOY BANKS.

No. 323. Bicycle Bank. Length, 11 in., height, 8 in., width 3½ in. As the crank is turned and the lever pressed, Prof. Pug Frog performs his great bicycle feat, and the coin placed on the bicycle is deposited in the bank. During the performance, Mother Goose gives attention to her melodies..per doz., $8 50

No. 225. Organ Bank, with revolving figure. Size, 4 in. high, 3½ wide, 2½ deep. Place the coin in the recess before the figure, and when the handle is turned a chime of bells will ring and the monkey will revolve and deposit the money in the bank. Appropriately decorated in colors, and packed one half dozen in a box........................per doz., $2 00

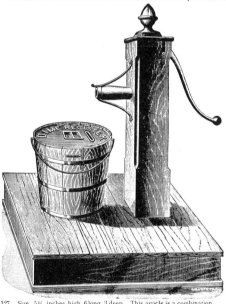

No. 116. Size, 6½ in. high, 4 wide, 3 deep. This bank is calculated to highly amuse children, as it is a musical toy as well as a savings bank. When the handle is turned a chime of bells will ring continuously, while at the same time the monkey will deposit in the bank any coins which may be placed on his tambourine, expressing his thanks by lifting his cap. Highly decorated, and packed one in a box..................................per doz., $4 00

No. 127. Size, 5½ inches high, 6 long, 3 deep. This article is a combination of a mechanical and registering bank. It is a very attractive novelty and cannot fail to please. The bucket is designed for dimes, in ordinary use only, and not for mutilated or old-fashioned coin of approximately the same size. Put a dime in the slot and push the pump handle up and down, when the amount will be correctly registered. When $5 have been deposited the lid of the bucket can be taken off; when replaced it is ready for business. If the directions pasted on the bottom of each bank are complied with, it cannot fail to work properly. Handsomely finished in nickel and wood colors, and packed one in a wooden box......................per doz., $8 5

160

TOY BANKS.

Minstrel Bank. The body of the bank is divided into two parts, the lower being the coin safe, while the upper part contains the mechanism for giving motion to the performers. A charge of one penny by the owner of a bank to see the performance will soon pay its cost. Each bank is tested and is known to be in proper working order before being packed at the factory...............................per doz., $9 00

No. 275. Cabin Bank; length 4¼ inches, height 3⅝ inches, width 3 inches. Place the coin upon the roof above the negro's head, move the handle of the white-wash brush, and the negro will be made to stand on his head and kick the coin into the bank, ¼ dozen in package..................per doz., $4 00

No. 1013. The Dairy; nickel finished, with brass bands, protected money slot, puzzle padlock; size 4 inches high, ½ dozen in package...................per doz., $4 50

No. 485. Presto Trick Bank, with lock and key opening; size 4½ inches high, 4 wide, 2½ deep. This bank contains the novel feature of a trick drawer. Press down the button over the front door, and the drawer will fly open. Put the coin in and close it. When the button is again pressed, the drawer will fly open, but the coin will have mysteriously disappeared. The money can be removed from the bottom of the bank by means of a lock and key. Handsomely decorated, and packed one-half dozen in a box...per doz., $2 25

No. 60. 5¼ inches, nickel plated.....................per doz., $9 00   No. 65, 5 inches, nickel plated.......................per doz., $8 00
The Bank of Columbia, constructed as near as possible on the plan of a real safe, with dials and handles on one side, Goddess of Liberty on the other, Uncle Sam with grip, marked "World's Fair."   No. 75 same as No. 65 but in old copper finish.....................per doz., $8 00

TOY BANKS AND WHEELTOY.

No. 300. Eagle Bank. Length, 8 inches; height, 6 inches; width, 4 inches. Place a coin in the Eagle's beak, press the lever, and the Eaglets rise from the nest crying for food. As the Eagle bends forward to feed them, the coin falls into the nest, and disappears in the receptacle below...per doz., $8 50

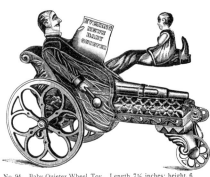

No. 94. Baby Quieter Wheel Toy. Length, 7½ inches; height, 6 inches; width, 3¾ inches. As the toy is drawn, each revolution of the wheels rings the bell and jumps the baby. Handsomely finished in fancy colors, ⅙ doz. in package...per doz., $4 25

No. 119. Organ Bank, with new dancing figures, complete with lock and key; size, 8½ inches high, 5½ wide, 3¾ deep. This handsomely finished bank has proven the most satisfactory article of the kind ever put on the market. It has very sweet chimes of bells, which sound when the handle is turned, and the monkey deposits all coin in the bank, and politely raises his cap, while the figures at his side revolve, producing a pleasing effect. Packed one in a wooden box.........................per doz., $8 00

No. 324. Cat and Mouse Bank. Height, 11½ inches; width, 5½ inches; depth, 4 inches. Place a coin in front of the mouse over the cat, press the lever, and as the coin disappears into the bank, the kitten, in fancy dress, appears, turning a somersault, holding the mouse and ball. Handsomely ornamented in fancy colors..............................per doz., $8 50

STEAM TOYS.

Excellent Show Pieces.

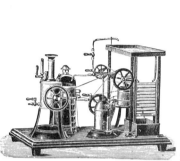

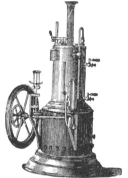

No. 411. Steam Engine, finished in brass, with whistle. per doz., $16 50

No. 421A. Steam Brewery, complete, with brass trimmed stationary engine..........per doz., $72 00

No. 107. Stationary Engine, extra fine, with double working cylinder, whistle and steam pipe, all complete, per doz.............................$120 00

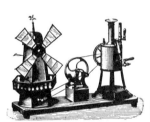

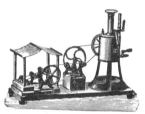

No. 116. Steam Windmill, with stationary engine, complete......per doz., $45 00

No. 423. Stationary Engine, with boiler, complete..................per doz., $45 00

No. 111. Steam Forge, with stationary steam engine, finished in brass, with whistle steam pipe........per doz., $27 00

No. 117. Steam Fountain, with stationary brass-finished engine........per doz., $45 00

No. 100. Stationary Engine, with polished brass boiler. per doz., $10 50

No. 121. Steam Dredge and Conveyor, with brass trimmed stationary engine, complete...........................per doz., $48 00

STEAM TOYS.

No. 128 B. Steam Propeller, complete with engine, finished in brass, 11 inches long..per doz., $15 00
No. 128. Same as above, 13 inches long...................... " " 24 00

No. 403 L. Steam Switch Locomotive with brass boiler, complete.........................per doz., $18 00

No. 126 A. Steam Switch Locomotive, with brass boiler, tender and whistle......................per doz., $48 00

No. 129. Steam Propeller with awning, complete with engine, finished in brass, 15¾ inches long.......................................per doz., $36 00
No. 191. Same as above with cabin, 15¾ inches long............. " " 72 00
No. 192. Same as above with two masts, compass, 19¾ in. long . " " 150 00

STEAM TRAINS WITH TRACKS.

No. 2. Steam Locomotive, track 3½ feet in diameter, in 9 sections, each 14 inches long, on which rails and sleepers are securely mounted, hinge lock on each section forming a solid track with a wooden base..........................per doz., $42 00
No. 26. Complete Train, consisting of locomotive with tender, 2 passenger cars and track..........................per doz., $90 00

No. 40. Complete Train, consisting of brass locomotive with tender, 2 passenger cars and track.................per doz., $42 00
No. 124 A. Complete Train, consisting of locomotive with tender, 2 passenger cars and track.......................per doz., $54 00

TOY STOVES.

NO. 10. JEWEL TOY RANGE.

No. 15. JEWEL TOY RANGE.

JEWEL TOY RANGE—TWO STYLES.

Price.

No. 10. Square top...each, $5 25
No. 15. With reservoir and high shelf... " 7 50

The above cuts show the two styles. This is undoubtedly the best and most handsome toy range made. In its mechanical construction it embraces all the practical features found in the larger ranges, being complete in all its working parts. Nickel plated doors, panels and edges, nickel plated legs, frame and ornamental high shelf. Cooking can be done upon this range. Each stove packed in a box with kettle, spider and cake griddle.

"THE O. K. No. 1" RANGE.

Length, 6¾ inches; height, 3⅞ inches; width, 5 inches; has 4 boiling holes, dumping grate, large fire box with door, oven with door, front door, draft damper openings; kettle, spider, baking pan, length of pipe and lifter included; each range is packed in a paper box, 1 dozen boxes in a large box, and 4 boxes in a crate...per doz., $6 50

THE "I. X. L." RANGE.

Length, 8¼ inches; height, 5¼ inches; width, 5½ inches; has 4 boiling holes, reservoir, dumping grate, large fire box, oven with door, front door, damper openings; kettle, spider, baking pan, griddle, length of pipe and lifter included; each range is packed in a paper box, 1 dozen boxes in large box, and 4 boxes in a crate..per doz., $9 00

THE "PET" RANGE.

Length, 11½ inches; height, 7 inches; width, 7 inches; har 4 boiling holes, reservoir, dumping grate. reservoir damper, large fire box with door, oven with door, front door with draft damper; large and small kettle, spider, baking pan, length of pipe and lifter included; each range is packed in a box, 1 dozen boxes in a crate.................................per doz., $18 00

THE "BABY" RANGE.

Length, 16 inches; height, 9¼ inches; width, 8¼ inches; has 6 boiling holes, reservoir, dumping grate, direct and reservoir dampers, large fire box with door, oven with door, front door with draft damper, and ash pit with door; kettle, spider, coffee pot, tea kettle, baking pan, length of pipe and lifter included; each range is packed in a box, ½ doz. boxes in a crate, per doz., $26 0

165

MECHANICAL TOYS.

No. 49-1. Mechanical bear........................per doz., $33 00

Mechanical mule clowns.......................................per doz., $33 00

No. 22-2. Mechanical dancer...................per doz., $24 00

Mechanical fire engine house with fire engine................per doz., $60 00

No. 49-7. Mechanical nurse....................per doz., $24 00

166

MECHANICAL TOYS.

No. 11–2. Mechanical Monkey, by clockwork,
per doz.....................................$33 00

Mechanical Cake Walk...per doz.,$33 00

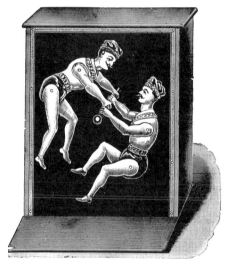

No. 32–9. Mechanical Clown Rider........per doz., $33 00

No. 49–16. Mechanical Acrobats, performing on bar.........per doz., $36 00

167

MECHANICAL LOCOMOTIVES.

No. 19-12. Locomotive, with tender, run by clock work; 14 in. long .... per doz., $21 00

No. 19-9. Iron locomotive, run by clock work; 7 inches long, per dozen .... $ 9 00

No. 19-10 Iron Locomotive and tender, run by clock work; 10½ inches long............................... per doz., $12 00

No. 19-11. Locomotive, run by clock work; 10 inches long, per dozen $16 00

IRON TOYS.

No. 6. Gondola Car, size to go with locomotive No. 1; 14 inches long, 3½ high....................................... per doz., $9 00

No. 1. True model of a modern style extension front locomotive, finished in colors, 16 wheels, all turn, 21 inches long with tender included.................................... per doz., $16 50

No. 3. Passenger Car, size to go with locomotive No. 1; 17 inches long, 4¾ high................................ per doz., $12 00

No. 2. Combination baggage, express and smoking car, size to go with locomotive No. 1; 17 inches long, 4¾ high....per doz., $12 00

No. 7. Caboose, finished in bright colors, to go with locomotive No 1; size, 7½x5½ inches .... per doz., $9 00

No. 4. Model Freight Car, 8 turning wheels made to the same gauge as locomotive and tender No. 1; size, 17 inches long, 4¾ high....................................... per doz., $12 00

MAGIC LANTERNS.

HELIO LANTERNS.

Extra fine quality, body polished Russia iron, duplex burners, contains 12 slides, 1 changeable landscape, 1 changeable comic picture, 1 chromotrope.

No. 782. Size ot lens 1¾.....per doz., $78 00
" 784. " " 2¼...... " " 120 00
" 786. " " 2¾...... " " 162 00

GLORIA LANTERNS.

Fine quality, body polished Russia iron, duplex burners, contains 12 slides, 1 chromotrope, 1 comic changeable picture, 1 changeable landscape.

No. 4 01. Lens 2 inches.....per doz., $90 00
" 4003. " 2⅜ " ...... " " 120 00
" 4005. " 3 " ...... " " 180 00

SCIOPTICON.

Finest magic lanterns, polished Russia iron, with a chromatic lens with thumbscrew, duplex burner, contains 24 slides, 1 chromotrope, 1 changeable comic picture, 1 changeable landscape.

No. 763. 4 inch lens.........per doz., $360 00

THE IMPROVED.

No. 624. Enameled Russia iron body, stands 18½ inches high, contains 12 slides, 1 chromotrope, 2 changeable pictures, duplex burners.....................................per doz., $126 00
No. 625. Same as above, one size larger.............. " " 180 00

THE IMPROVED.

No. 622. Enameled Russia iron, brass mounted body, triplex burner, stands 24½ inches high, contains 12 slides, 6 changeable pictures, 2 chromotropes....................per doz., $300 00

VIEWS FOR MAGIC LANTERNS.

Glass slides, hand painted colored pictures, will fit corresponding diameter of lenses.

No. 3. 1¼ inches diameter, 1 doz. in package.......per doz., $ 60 | No. 6. 2⅛ inches diameter, 1 doz. in package.........per doz., $1 50
" 4. 1½ " " 1 " " .... " " 60 | " 7. 2½ " " 1 " " .... " " 2 00
" 3½. 1⅜ " " 1 " " .... " " 60 | " 8. 3⅛ " " 1 " " .... " " 2 65
" 4½. 1¾ " " 1 " " .... " " 75 | " 9. 3½ " " 1 " " .... " " 3 00
" 5. 2 " " 1 " " .... " " 1 00 | " 10. 4 " " 1 " " .... " " 4 00

MAGIC LANTERNS.

CLIMAX.

Painted red, wood cabinet double doors, containing six slides and three rotary slides.

No. 1231C. Size of lens 1 inch..per doz. $13 50
No. 1233C.   "   "   1½ " ..   "   21 00

No. 1800. Painted red, in wood case with handle, contains 12 slides, per doz..........................$12 00
No. 40. Painted red, in wood case with handle, contains 12 slides, 2 changeable pictures, 1 chromotrope, lens 1½ inches..per doz., $24 00

BALL SHAPED LANTERN.

Painted red, double door, wood case.

No. 532C. Size of lens 1 inch, contains 10 slides, per doz......................................$12 00
No. 535C. Size of lens 1¼ inch, contains 10 slides, per doz................................... 16 50

SQUARE SHAPED LANTERN.

Polished Russia Iron, Brass trimmings in double door, wood box.

No. 1757. Contains 8 slides, 1 chromotrope, 1 changeable picture, 1 mechanical picture, size of lens 1⅝ inches........per doz., $42 00

OBLONG SHAPED LANTERN.

Painted body, in double door wood case, contains 10 slides.

No. 524C. Size of lens 1 inch.........................per doz., $12 00
No. 529C. Size of lens 1½ inch.......................   "   18 00

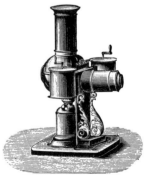

BRASS CLIMAX.

Polished brass body, contains 4 slides, 6 circular pictures, 2 changeable pictures.

No. 648. Size of lens 1¼ inch..per doz., $24 00

THE POPULAR LANTERN.

Painted body, neatly packed.

No. 523. Contains 6 slides, size of lens 1 inch....................per doz., $4 50
No. 524. Contains 12 slides, size of lens 1 inch....................per doz., $8 00
No. 527. Contains 12 slides, size of lens 1¼ inch.................per doz., $12 00

ROTATING MAGIC LANTERN.

Contains 100 pictures on rollers.

No. 206.........................per doz., $42 00

CLIPS AND SPINDLES.

No. 5128. Letter Clip, maroon
finish, 1 doz. in box, per
doz $0 80

SPENCERIAN HORSE
SHOE CLIPS.

No. 5136. Letter Clips, 12 in box, maroon
finish.........................per doz., $1 00

Small ....per doz., $0 45
Medium.............   "   75
Large...............   "   1 20

No. 5424. Letter File, 12 in box, maroon
finish......................... per doz., $0 60
No. 5408. Letter File, maroon finish, 6 in a
box ....per doz.,   85

TWINE HOLDERS.

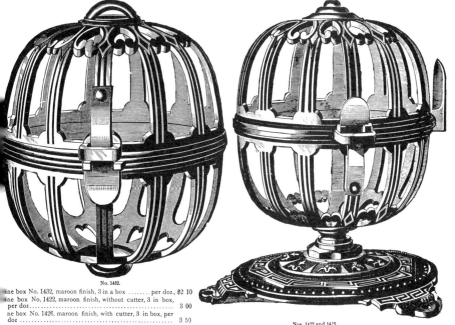

No. 1432.

ine box No. 1432, maroon finish, 3 in a box ....per doz., $2 10
ine box No. 1422, maroon finish, without cutter, 3 in box,
    per doz..   3 00
ne box No. 1426, maroon finish, with cutter, 3 in box, per
    doz 3 50

Nos. 1422 and 1423.

171

INK STANDS AND PAPER WEIGHTS.

TRAVELING INKS.

No. 3208-2. Assorted,
6 in box.... per box, $3 00
No. 463-0. Assorted,
per doz............. 3 75
No. 463-2. Assorted,
per doz............. 5 75

No. 19. Assorted, ½ doz. in
box..............per doz., $3 75

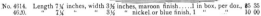

No. 4614. Length 7¼ inches, width 3½ inches, maroon finish.....1 in box, per doz., $5 35
4620. " 7¼ " " 3½ " nickel or blue finish, 1 " " 10 00

No. 4097. Size, 8x6 inches, maroon finish, brass pen rack ....per doz., $6 25

No. 22-24. Assorted ½ doz. in box,
per doz $3 85

No. 4352. Length, 9 inches, width, 6½ inches, ebony and gold finish, brass pen racks.....per doz., $9 50

No. 13. Assorted fancy colors, ½ doz.
in box ....p r doz., $1 50

GLASS PAPER WEIGHTS.

No. 108. Assorted ½ doz. in box,
per doz........................ $3 85

No. 106. Assorted ½ doz. in box,
per doz $3 00

INK STANDS.

No 4344. Length 5 inches width 3½ inches, maroon finish, 3 in a box...per doz., $2 00

No. 4436. Length 4 inches, width 2½ inches, maroon finish, 3 in a box...per doz., $2 15

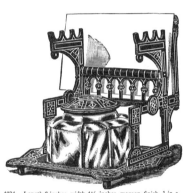

No 4606. Length 5 inches, width 3½ inches, maroon finish, 1 in a box...per doz., $2 90

No. 4634. Length 6 inches, width 4½ inches, maroon finish, 1 in a box...per doz., $4 25

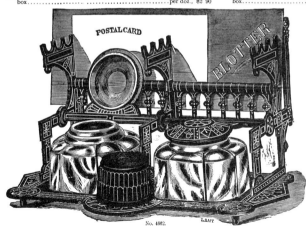

No. 4662.   L.SAFF

GLASS INK STANDS.

2 inches square, ½ dozen in box, doz...................... $2 00
2½ inches square, ⅓ dozen in box, per doz.................. 3 75
2¼ inches square, 1-6 dozen in box, per doz............. 5 00
2 inches square, double, 1-6 doz. in box, per doz 6 00

No. 4656. One well only, length 8 inches, nickel and blue finish, with penwiper.....per doz., $15 00
No. 4662. Length 9 inches, width 5 inches, nickel and blue finish, with penwiper, per doz., 18 00
No. 4642. Length 9 inches, width 5 inches, maroon finish, two wells................per doz., 8 50

173

WRITING FLUIDS AND COPYING INKS.

COPYING INK.

One bottle in a wood box.

Quarts.........................per doz., $8 50
Pints............................ "   5 60
½ pints......................... "   3 50

One bottle in a wood box.

Writing Fluid, quarts......per doz., $5 50
 "   "   pints........ "   3 50
 "   "   ½ " .... "   2 25

One dozen in a wood box.

Writing Fluid, ½ pints.....per doz., $1 75

One bottle in a wood box.

Compound Writing and Copying, quarts,
  per doz.............................$7 50

174

DOLLS.

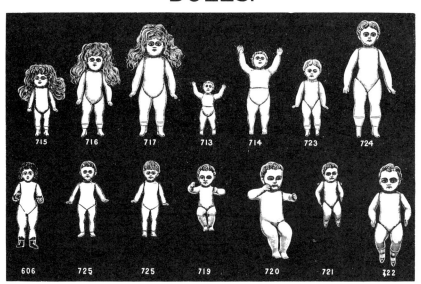

BISQUE BABIES, SWIMMERS, WILL FLOAT.

No. 713. 2¾ inches, 1 dozen in package...............per doz., $0 75
" 714. 4¼ " 1 " " " .... " 1 75

WIRE JOINTED BABIES IN BISQUE.

No. 723. 3¼ inches, 1 dozen in package ....per doz., $0 88
" 724. 5¼ " ½ " " " .... " 2 00

BISQUE BABIES WITH FLOWING HAIR, PAINTED SHOES, JOINTED ARMS.

No. 715. 3½ inches, 1 dozen in package ....per doz., $0 75
" 716. 4¼ " 1 " " " .... " 1 25
" 717. 5½ " 1 " " " .... " 1 75

BOYS JOINTED IN BISQUE, SITTING POSITIONS.

No. 721. 3 inches, 1 dozen in package..................per doz., $0 75
" 722. 5 " ½ " " " .... " 2 00

SAME AS ABOVE, NOT JOINTED.

No. 719. 3¼ inches, 1 dozen in package ....per doz., $0 75
" 720. 4¼ " 1 " " " .... " 1 75

SAME, STANDING POSITIONS, ASSORTED.

No. 725. 3¼ inches, ½ gross in package.............per gross, $10 50

BISQUE BABIES.

No. 610.

All Bisque jointed body, natural glass eyes, flowing hair, painted shoes.

No. 718. Length 4 inches, 1 dozen in box....per doz., $1 75
" 608. " 5½ " 1 " " " ... " 2 00
" 610. " 6¼ " ½ " " " ... " 3 50

Same as Nos. 718 to 610, but with teeth and moving eyes.

No. 611. Length 5¼ inches, ½ dozen in box....per doz., $4 00
" 612. " 6¼ " ½ " " " ... " 6 00
" 613. " 9 " 1 6 " " " ... " 8 50

175

DOLLS.

No. 0

No. 800 to 802.

ENGLISH RAG DOLLS.

Best quality indestructible dolls, linen faces, glass eyes, fancy dresses, soft arms and limbs, dressed in costumes, "Little Red Riding Hood," "Bo Peep," "Blue Eyes," "Dew Drop."

No. 00.	13½ inches long,	⅓ dozen in package	......per doz.,	$4 00
0.	15	"	"	⅓	" " "	....	" "	6 00
1.	17	"	"		...........................••.....	" "	8 00
2.	19	"	"		....	" "	12 00

WASHABLE DOLLS.

Extra size heads, with teeth, glass eyes, lace trimmed chemise, imitation shoes and stockings, soft limbs. The popular line.

No. 800.	18	inches.	1 dozen in packages	..........per doz.,	$2 00
801.	22	"	½ " "	....	" "	3 50
802.	29½	"	⅓ " "	....	" "	8 00

WASHABLE DOLLS, EXTRA QUALITY.

Washable heads, glass eyes, mohair hair dressings, fancy chemises, bare feet.

No. 803.	17½ inches,	1 dozen in package	..........per doz.,	$2 00
804.	23½	"	½ " " "	....	" "	3 50
805.	27½	"	⅓ " " "	....	" "	6 50
806.	30	"	⅙ " " "	....	" "	9 00

FINE WASHABLE DOLLS.

Fine washable heads, fine waved hairdressing, full lace chemise, trimmed with bows, fine double stitched body, glazed limbs and arms.

No. 766. 23½ inches, ⅓ dozen in package............per doz., $8 50

WASHABLE DOLLS.

"Papa and Mama."

No. 808. 14 inches, 1 dozen in package...............per doz., $2 00

"Fat Baby."

No. 807. 13 inches, 1 dozen in package...............per doz., $2 00

BOY WASHABLE DOLLS.

Washable heads, glass eyes, boy hair dressings, fancy shirts, bare feet.

No. 809.	17½ inches	1 dozen in package	..........per doz.,	$2 00
541.	16	"	½ " " "	....	" "	4 00

BOY WASHABLE DOLLS.

Fine washable heads, glass eyes, new side-parted hairdressing, bosom front shirt with bow, bare feet.

No. 797.	16 inches,	½ dozen in package	..........per doz.,	$4 75
798.	20½	"	⅓ " " "	....	" "	6 00

Fine grade wig, natural lamb's wool, fine body and shirt.

No. 799. 16 inches, ½ dozen in package..............per doz., $3 75

No, 804 to 806.

No. 808.

No. 809.

176

JAPANESE SCREENS.

We carry a complete assortment of Japanese Folding Screens in choice designs and colors.   Also a good assortment of Japanese Fire Screens.

PERFUMERY.

No. 4007.   The Vandalia Toilet Perfume Pitcher........per doz., $2 00

No. 4136.   Beautidora, exact size, ½-dozen in box.......per doz., $2 25

No. 1176½. Rajah Ash Receiver, per doz., $2 00

No. 1296.   Lamp, Extract
1 doz. in box...per doz., $2 00

No. 1102.   Duck in the Pond, Novelty Extract, per doz., $2 25

PERFUMERY.

No. 3439. Half-ounce size, one dozen in box..per doz.,$0 40 net.

E. W. Hoyt's German Cologne

Trial, or 25 cent size, per doz., $1 75 net.
Medium, or 50 cent " " 3 75 "
Large, or $1 00 " " 7 50 "

Fac-Simile of Bottle.

Tappan's aroma cologne, small size, one dozen in box, per doz., net..................$0 75

No. 1542. One doz. in package, ½ ounce German cologne, per doz......$0 85 net.

No. 4325. Rometta, exact size, ½ dozen in box........per doz., $2 00

No. 3771. Invincible cologne jug, 4¾ inches high, ½ dozen in box...per doz., $2 00

179

PERFUMERY.

No. 4302. Brilliant, exact size, ⅙ doz in box........per doz., $4 25

No. 402. Columbus extract.........................per doz., $2 25

No. 1459. Fine double extracts, assorted odors, 1 doz. in box......per doz., $2 00

Blue Lilies and Bouquet Regale, 8-oz. bottles, per bottle, net................$2 00

No. 1475. Tonquin Musk, exact size, 1 doz. in box, per doz......................$1 00

Exact Size.

No. 4063. Perfume bottle holder of finest French bisque, a grotesque and pretty ornament and match receiver, a bottle of good perfume in each, one dozen in box.....per doz., $2 00

PERFUMERY.

Exact Size.

No. 4135. The Napoleon Perfume Pitcher, with Ground Glass Stoppers, filled with first-rate perfume, beautiful also as an oil or vinegar cruet for the table. One-third dozen in box...................per doz., $3 00

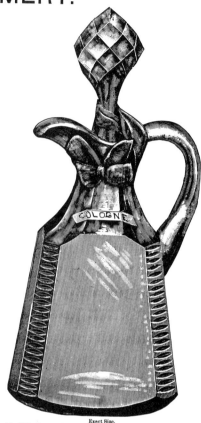

Exact Size.

No. 4324. Immaculate, 1-6 dozen in box............per doz., $6 00

No. 44. Little Folks.—Size 3x5 inches an attractive and ready selling novelty two bottles of perfume and one fancy satin sachet bag, in handsome box. Price, per doz. boxes...................................$2 00

No. 1214¼. Nickeled fancy framed 3x5 inches with colored picture under glass, 1 bottle of perfume. per doz.... ....$0 85

No. 901. Novelty Perfume Basket 1 doz. in box. per doz. $0 75

PERFUMERY.

No. 434. Perfume Bisque, 4¼ inches high, handsome Bisque match safe, assorted figures, with bottle of fragrant perfume, packed 1 dozen to each box, per doz., $2 00

Exact size.

No. 4048. La France perfume flagon, with choice lily of the valley decorations, filled with fine handkerchief extracts, assorted odors, one dozen in box..... per doz., $2 00

No. 4321. 2-ounce size, ½ dozen in box, per doz.......................$2 00

No. 946. Aladdin's fairy lamp, 1 dozen in box....per doz., $2 00

No. 4123. Ding dong crystal bell, exact size, ½ dozen in box.......................per doz., $1 75

PERFUMERY.

No. 490.   Moss vase.................per doz., $2 00

Exact size.

No. 4130. Sultana, new perfume bottle; a new
and pretty glass stoppered bottle, filled
with excellent perfume, half dozen in box,
per doz................................. $2 00

Fac-simile, medium size.

No. 4139. The new perfume bottle Mystic Circle, with a **new**
and very effective decoration,
and glass stopper to match.
Filled with first-rate handkerchief perfume, each size, ½
dozen in box...... per doz., $2 00

No. 4320. Exact size, 1 dozen in a box, glass bouquet
holder, nickel-framed compass and bottle of
perfume ....per doz., $2 00

No. 4194. Union square, 2-oz. size,
½ dozen in a box.....per doz., $2 00

No. 4312. Montrose, exact size, 1 dozen
in box................. per doz., $2 00

PERFUMERY.

No. 4316. Six-oz. size, ⅙ dozen in a
box......................per doz., $3 75

No. 4121. Our nosegay the new perfume holder of finest
crystal glass, fire polished, filled with good handkerchief perfume, a new, novel and beautiful article, half
dozen in box...............................per doz., $2 00

Exact Size.

No. 4230. Utopia, ½ doz. in box, per doz., $2 75

Exact Size.

No. 301. Willow Chair.—5 inches high, a very
attractive novelty, each chair decorated with
violets, holding one bottle of elegant perfume.
Price per dozen chairs....................$2 25

No. 3394. Pearl Flower Vase, one doz.
in box.............. ....per doz., $2 00

Exact Size.

No. 4137. Prism Bud, 1 doz. in box........per doz., $1 50

Exact Size.

184

PERFUMERY.

No. 53. Horseshoe perfume per doz $0 50

No. 3709. Tippecanoe china jug, assorted colors, filled with handkerchief perfume, one dozen in box ....per doz., $1 00

No. 992. Fine decorated jug, per doz $2 00

ACTUAL SIZE

No. 1090. Beautiful imported candlestick with bronze arms and holders for candlestick, packed 1 in a box, per doz $1 25

No. 460. Decorated vase, size, 2½x3½ inches, richly ornamented in gilt, filled with delicate perfume, packed ½ dozen in each box.... per doz., $2 25

No. 3383. Handy Tulip vase, exact size, 1 dozen in a box...... per doz., $0 75

No. 4059. Maywood, exact size, ½ dozen in box, per doz $2 25

PERFUMERY.

No. 3774. 4¼ inches high, prismatic jug, ½ doz. in box, per doz................................ ....$2 25

No. 1278. Cornucopia, per doz. $2 00

No. 1281. Fine ornamental glass bottle, 7 inches high, per doz., $2 00

No. 4128. Canterbury, exact size, ½ dozen in box, per doz..................................$2 25

Exact size.

No. 4068. "Tit willow" perfume jug, fine majolica, bas-relief decorations, a beautiful little novelty, filled with fine handkerchief perfume, one dozen in box...........per doz., net, $0 40

No. 191 Novelty perfume, per doz., net...............................$0 75

No. 420. Perfume bisque, 4¼ inches high, handsome Bisque match safe, assorted girl and boy, with bottle delicate perfume, packed one dozen to each box...........per doz., $2 00

PERFUMERY.

Exact Size.

No. 3900. Still alarm, 1 doz. in box, per doz., $1 75

Exact Size.

No. 4184. Sunbeam, half dozen in box . . . . .per dozen $2 00

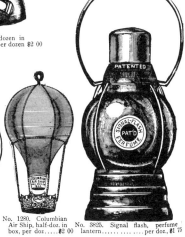

Exact Size.

No. 4078. Reflector Perfume lantern, white and green globes, assorted in box, filled with first-rate perfume, one dozen in box . . . . .per doz., $0 75

Exact Size.

No. 1891. "Sparkler" perfumery lantern, green and red assorted in box; "as pretty as a picture" filled with good perfume; the globe of the green lantern is of green glass; a beautiful little novelty that sells well in any trade; packed one dozen in box . . . . .per doz., $0 75

No. 220. Merchants' Dispatch. 1 doz. in box, per doz., net $0 50

No. 1280. Columbian Air Ship, half-doz. in box, per doz. $2 00

No. 3825. Signal flash, perfume lantern . . . . .per doz., $1 75

187

BIBLIOGRAPHY

The Look of the Old West   Foster–Harris, Viking Press

World Book Encyclopedia

Treasury of Frontier Relics   Les Beitz; Edwin House

Wishbook 1865   Blumenstein, Old Time Bottle Publishing Co.

Treasure Hill   Jackson; University of Arizona Press

Marshall Field & Co., Illustrated Catalogue

INDEX

189

191

For other books on collecting, write for free illustrative brochure.

OLD TIME BOTTLE PUBLISHING COMPANY

Department L

611 Lancaster Dr., N.E.

Salem, Oregon 97301

Telephone:

Area Code 503

362-1446